Emotional
COMMON
SENSE

Revised Edition

Emotional COMMON SENSE

Avoiding Self-Destructiveness
and Enhancing
Personal Development

ROLLAND S. PARKER

HARPER & ROW, PUBLISHERS, New York
Cambridge, Hagerstown, Philadelphia, San Francisco,
London, Mexico City, São Paulo, Sydney

Library of Congress Cataloging in Publication Data

Parker, Rolland S
  Emotional common sense.
  Bibliography: p.
  Includes index.
  1. Self-destructive behavior. 2. Emotions.
3. Interpersonal relations. 4. Conduct of life.
I. Title.
RC569.5.S45P37 1981   158'.1   80-8214
ISBN 0-06-013298-1   81 82 83 84 85 10 9 8 7 6 5 4 3 2 1
ISBN 0-06-464046-9 (pbk.)   81 82 83 84 85 10 9 8 7 6 5 4 3 2 1

For Irmgard

I feel, therefore I am

Contents

Preface to the Revised Edition

This book is the expression of the struggles and solutions shared by over 10,000 people in my Human Relations Workshops through many years, experiences in intensive psychotherapy and career counseling with clients, the writings of scientists, psychotherapists, and other thinkers about human nature, and certainly my personal struggle towards emotional fulfillment. The topics are those which frequently concern people. As in the first edition, I pledged to myself that I would tell it the way it is, that I would be truthful to the point of bluntness about the way people often behave—sometimes nobly and intelligently, but frequently with base motives, ludicrously, and without self-respect.

Emotional Common Sense acknowledges the complexity of human nature. It would be dishonest to offer stereotyped solutions for everybody without regard for individuality. The body of learning about people continues to grow, and my own ideas have developed. Therefore, the second edition has at least 80 percent new text, and almost all of the scientific references are from the last five years.

Unnecessary self-destructiveness remains a central theme, but there are many new sections about fear of success, the masochistic attitude which causes us to stage-manage disaster for our lives, depression, stress, anger, understanding our identity, etc. One of my favorite ideas is still offered a place of honor: the "Ouch Principle." If somebody steps on your toes, say "Ouch!" All too frequently, we permit people to degrade us, and then offer truly marvelous justifications to let ourselves be pushed around. I suggest that we get rid of those who are deliberately troublesome. That's when the fun begins in a discussion, since there are always people who object to this idea. Another theme which distinguishes this book is the importance of seeking solutions which evolve from your identity, your uniqueness as an individual. Correct decisions about life (mate, career, etc.) evolve from knowing who you really are, what you can reasonably do, and then pursuing personal goals without too much self-indulgence. I even suggest that the principles of emotional common sense will speed up psychotherapy by helping you to determine the key issues in your own life, so that you can avoid getting caught up in some pet ideas automatically applied by a psychotherapist with a narrow point of view.

Many people have contributed to this volume. I want to acknowledge, first of all, my valued editor Harold Grove, who also contributed his talents to the first edition. Bertha Klausner, literary agent and friend, has encouraged my career as a writer. Another close friend, Jane Morrin, made a vital contribution to the success of the Human Relations Workshops, from which so much of this book evolved.

R.S.P.

New York City
January 1981

Emotional COMMON SENSE

1) Recognizing Self-Destructiveness

Most of us create situations and relationships which damage our peace of mind and ability to achieve deeply desired goals. I would bet that you are committed right now to some avoidable error. Some of your habits and attitudes will predictably bring you into defeat and self-reproach. You would probably even defend your self-destructive position!

Do you self-destruct? Do you have the sneaking suspicion that you are the victim of your own foolishness? Do you victimize yourself and add to life's inevitable traumas? Does a new situation "zap" your stomach with fear, even before you get to bat? When you are alone, do you have gloomy thoughts and despair about the future?

Can you identify with these statements?

- "I feed myself negative talk."
- "I feel damaged."
- "I have to keep my self-destructiveness, because if I change, nobody will want me."
- "She hangs on to her neurosis like a treasure."

I define *self-destructiveness* as creating, tolerating, defending, and continuing actions which bring us into situations that we swear that we want to avoid.

Emotional common sense, on the other hand, is using our self-understanding to avoid destructive actions, to stage-manage constructive actions, and to associate only with people with whom we can exchange positive experiences.

The first step in overcoming self-destructiveness is acknowledging that it is part of your personality. Strangely enough, some people seem to crave it, like the person who said, "My blood was being sucked. Custom caused me to let it continue."

ARE YOU SELF-DESTRUCTIVE?

If you were to think about all the things you have done today and yesterday, would you come to the conclusion that everything you have done is in your own best interest? I would probably win a bet that some pleasure or casual action violated some goal or value, or created a problem with somebody whose affection or goodwill was important.

Self-destructiveness is more than killing oneself, though this can be the end result of an unhappy lifestyle. It is also:

- Antagonizing somebody important
- Permitting people to influence us unwisely
- Letting clutchers deplete us
- Accepting unreal obligations
- Tolerating emotional pain
- Self-hatred and lack of self-acceptance and self-respect
- Losing self-assertiveness through excessive dependence
- Excessively critical attitudes toward others
- Inability to express our needs for support and love
- Inability to express pain or anger
- Inviting disaster through dishonesty
- Creating a hostile world around us
- Harboring unrealistic feelings of guilt
- Neglecting to build up an important relationship
- Not listening to others' needs and messages
- Seeing oneself as valueless
- Becoming a self-selected wallflower.

Taking the easy way out. The difference between emotional common sense and self-destructiveness is more than awareness of light and dark. Dedication to improving the quality of your life really involves self-discipline and efforts to improve your personality. Self-discipline? Yes. It is not a popular idea these days. I own a whole library of books on psychology, psychiatry, psychotherapy, and psychoanalysis. The only time that "self-discipline" appeared was a misprint! For curiosity, I examined the indexes of ten different books on the subject of how to conduct psychotherapy. What did I find? Self-fulfillment, self-acceptance, self-esteem—all very good to have, but not easily achieved if you are in the habit of taking the easy way out.

Improving your life does require making a careful survey of how you allocate your resources. Do your friends consume your money, spirit, time, and vitality in ways that offer you little and distract from deeply felt goals and wishes? Do you set tasks for yourself that are so difficult that eventually you cannot bear the thought of them? The result is years of self-recrimination for having accomplished nothing. Nothing else you do can be enjoyed because of the thought of the malignant task.

Destructiveness to others. Have you ever been fired or bereaved or failed an assignment, and then wondered why no one was available to share your suffering? Have you wondered why an employee you have been overbearing with reported a failure of yours or did not cover up a mistake when the top boss came down for an inspection? Are you a surprised lover or spouse who is suffering from the long-concealed rage that is finally being expressed to you? It *is* self-destructive to participate in the destruction of others. It is self-destructive to nag, withdraw support from, and criticize some human being who deserves or expects some support or warmth from you.

Passive passivity. Did you stand by quietly while our human and economic resources were being squandered in Vietnam? Perhaps you feel that public transportation is scandalously inadequate? Did the telephone company turn off your service and then charge you to restore it? Did an employee of some private company or governmental agency neglect your interest or abuse you when you needed service? Yes; oh, you did nothing about it! You didn't sign a petition, or join a political club, or write to a newspaper, or ask to see the clod's supervisor? You are found guilty of the crime against yourself of self-destructiveness. Next case.

Employment. You are underpaid? Too bad. Your supervisor plays favorites? That's dreadful. The owner of the company is skimming off the profits and not paying taxes? Awful. Your boss shouts at you and humiliates you in public? Terrible. You know that you are creative and you must do repetitive work? How ghastly. You wish you had more skills so that you could be assigned to that other fascinating department? That would be grand. Passed over for promotion? Tough. If any of these items are true for you and you have made no changes, you deserve it because you are either lazy, cowardly, or stupid. No? Oh, now I understand. You undergo abuse because you think you need security. The truth is that you are self-destructive.

Intimate relationships. By the way, how is your sex life? Are you having the kind of warm, vital experience you have longed for since those wet-dreaming, grubby, pawing days of your uneducated, yearning adolescence? *No?* I see. Your partner wasn't so hot, and you told him (her) so in no uncertain terms:

• "Well, my beddytime pal tries very hard, but I like a good fight before I'll yield myself."
• "No, it isn't *that* way with me, but he wants to do that really dirty thing to me."
• "Well, everything else about our relationship is all right, but my wife isn't very sexual and I have this great big need to have my masculinity confirmed, so I'll drop her and get someone better."
• "My story is different. My husband is not patient with me. I know I've been married for years, but he really should give me more time to adjust."
• "Well, I feel differently. But even though I just adore sex, I would feel like a slut if I ever let go. After all, really nice women don't move and make all those disgusting noises."
• "My girl is very passionate, but it takes me forty-five seconds to climax, and she isn't satisfied. I think that if she were normal she could climax twice with all that fooling around beforehand. Did I seek therapy? No, why should I? That's for sickies."
• "I don't need marital therapy. I need a loan. My wife is pregnant. She told me she just knew she couldn't get pregnant that time of the month."

Let's have a checkup on your feelings. "Why bother? I trust my feelings." Oh, yeah, I've been watching you. Your boss abuses you, your mate puts you down, your friends kid you, and you never learned how to say "ouch." As for *you*—yes, you, over there in the corner. When you get irritated, there is no stopping you. You with your loud voice and insensitive tongue. Just because your mother/father abused the family doesn't give you a license to cut everybody to shreds. Oh? This is a dog-eat-dog world? You don't want anybody nibbling at your bones? OK. Just go around with your hands guarding the family jewels, because you are really well loved, you self-destructive lout!

Health. And, my friend, how are you taking care of yourself? Exercise? "Got too many things to do." Vitamins? "Nah, I eat a healthy diet of french-fried potatoes, Fritos, and pork chops." Overweight? "You have no idea how unhappy I get late at night." Relaxation? "I'm too tense." Sunshine? "No, there is a great new carcinogenic compound that gives me really a marvelous tan without even going out." Medical checkup? "Next summer when I'm not so busy." Vague pain in the tummy? "Listen, those doctors don't know anything. They can't be trusted." "Hey, you left me out. I don't brush my teeth or wash my hands after going to the bathroom, because my father insisted on it years ago." Which of these self-destructive attitudes are yours?

How are you handling your money? You or your ever-loving are spending your most productive hours/days/weeks/months/years/decades earning it. Answer the question. Don't look away.

• "Well, my wife drove me into debts which are equal to over two years' earnings before taxes. Cancel her credit cards? Are you crazy? She wouldn't like that. Besides, she might insist that I have sex with her more often than once every two weeks." Well, what's so terrible about that? "Oh, I never liked her."

• You over there? "I lost my job because of embezzlement. My wife is insecure and she really needed that grandiose house to live in. As for me, it isn't so inappropriate for a fine fellow like me, either."

• "Can I get into this? I had this swell firm. I stole a great idea from my employer, who was really a crook in the way he handled his clients. I then started opening offices all over the East Coast while the recession was growing worse. I knew the economy was bound to turn around. Why should I listen to negative advice from my employees? Listen, I'm smarter than anyone."

Well, what happened to it? Come on. "Oh, yeah, one of them did win a suit against me when I didn't want to pay him vacation wages. A couple of clients also pushed me out of business."

• "This conversation is making me edgy. It seems that I had all my money tied up in the market when everything went down. Funny thing. You know that broker who put me into Interplanetary Packaging? I never heard from him."

Keep it up fellows, welfare is very popular. A few new cases won't be noticed. And as for you, madam, you may think that your daughter loves you because you give her everything she wants. Remember, when her husband kicks her out on her expensively clothed rear, you will be supporting her again, and also a couple of emotionally starved grandchildren.

Are you seeking a mate? (I'd like to hear a few words from you eager lovers.) "Well, I'm getting married because that's the only way I'll ever get her to bed." "Well, I don't want to be the only girl left unmarried on the block. You should hear my mother nag me about wanting grandchildren." "Say, what's wrong about getting married because I'm lonely, pregnant, hard up, jealous, avaricious, guilt-ridden, passive, aggressive, sado-masochistic, dependent?" There is nothing wrong with any of these reasons for marriage except self-destructiveness.

• "I'm none of these things, but I have one hell of a time finding my mate. I don't know what I'm doing wrong. Why do I meet all these creeps? After all, I advertise in a magazine that is sold on the newsstands. Lots of people can find out about me. I go into bars that are really crowded. I know, I get stuck next to some loser all night and can't move even if I try. I even sleep with everybody I meet so I can really get to know them."

• "I'm different. I don't sleep with anybody I've just met. I really have to know somebody very well before I'll let them even touch me."

• "As for me, I like to go out with a dozen girls simultaneously. That way I can really compare them. True, I am a little tired after a week of sex, but when the one comes along who is really meant for me I will really know."

• "You have it all wrong. You have to read their horoscope. There was the dreamiest guy, but when I found out he was a

Taurus—and I am a Leo—that really turned me off. You know how *they* mix."

• "Well, astrology is all right, but my guy is going to have to be the right religion. You should have heard my mother when she found out that I went out with a Jew/Catholic/Protestant/Black/White/Redskin/Japanese."

• "Let me tell you about my mother. Even though she mistreated me when I was a child, I feel that now that she is in her sixties and doesn't have a chance for any more happiness, I am not entitled to any either, so I only associate with undesirables."

If your choice of a mate lacks emotional common sense, you will deserve your fate, whether you selected or rejected someone for foolish reasons.

Accepting bad treatment. I enjoy stirring up a workshop or lecture by making the following statement: "It is absolutely justifiable to dump anybody who is destructive to us." Invariably, somebody will justify why we should hang around while being cut to shreds. Maybe it is a parent, a grown child, an employer, a friend, you name it. Why don't you ask yourself how many people in your life really ought to be sent into outer space? Now, think about a couple of people who damage you. Can you justify remaining with them. Yes? If so, I insist that you finish this book. However, if you have decided to drop a few abusive creeps, you have received the message, and you don't have to read further. No, you can't get a refund, because you already have your money's worth.

Self-dislike. The important difference between those who tolerate or create unhappy lives and those who are successful and happy (by their own standards) is how they regard themselves. It could be called "masochism" versus "optimism." The situation is more complicated than "losers" versus "winners," although this is how people often label themselves.

A feeling of comfort with yourself should be somewhat independent of external rewards. Since there is little justice in this life, to expect that virtue and hard work will inevitably result in prosperity, victory, and admiration is foolish. There is very little room at the top. Consequently, to devote one's entire life to raising self-esteem through always being a "winner" is predictably self-destructive. I am not minimizing the importance of investing ourselves in hard work. Rather, our self-love must be more basic, and not shaken by lack of appreciation after an honorable effort.

VICTIM OR VICTOR

Please think carefully, and with courage, about this self-assessment. Are you closer in your attitude to the masochist or to the optimist?

Masochist

- *Self-destructive*: Creating unpleasant moods and situations
- *Maladaptive:* Repeating bad experiences
- *Pessimistic*: Expecting the worst
- *Masochistic*: Putting up with the garbage handed to you
- *Imprudent*: Antagonizing people
- *Static*: Not growing and developing
- *Dependent*: Upset unless others take care of you
- *Incompetent*: Unable to do or to learn what is important
- *Lonely*: Craving company but not trying to get it
- *Lacking foresight*: Making avoidable mistakes
- *Stage-managing defeat*: Avoiding failure rather than creating success
- *Inner conflicts*: Unable to decide what you really want out of life
- *Lacking identity*: Not knowing who you are and what is suitable for you
- *Fear of success*: Getting nervous and retreating when things go well
- *Self-hating*: Feeling unworthy and not entitled to anything good
- *Passive*: Letting things happen while others get the goodies.

Optimist

- *Constructive*: Creating pleasures in accord with deeply felt values
- *Adaptive*: Learning from experience
- *Optimistic*: Taking risks because you believe things will go well
- *Self-respecting*: Refusing to let others mistreat you; you feel entitled to rewards and good treatment
- *Prudent*: Creating allies and mentors

- *Creative*: Looking at the world a little differently than you used to and being emotionally self-reliant
- *Autonomous*: Enjoying your personality
- *Competent*: Knowing how to get things done
- *Social*: Enjoying people
- *Foresight*: Looking ahead to avoid mistakes
- *Stage-managing success*: Planning for what will work and not just avoiding failure
- *Integrated*: All your efforts enhance each other
- *Positive identity*: You like who you are
- *Expecting success*: Projects are organized to win, not to avoid failure
- *Active*: Influencing events to your advantage.

YOUR SELF-EVALUATION

If you were to see somebody doing things, feeling, and talking like you, what would you say about him/her? If the answer is that such a person is behaving against his best interests, that the effects he has on those he loves or needs or wishes respect from are poor, then you, the reader, lack *emotional common sense*. Perhaps your reaction is that of the self-destructive masochist. It is my plan to help you toward self-understanding by reviewing the key areas in which self-destructiveness violates emotional common sense.

2) Identification and Self-Destruction

The first step in developing emotional common sense is to develop a clearer picture of ourselves, to understand how it develops, and to appreciate the effect that it has on how we act and our well-being. Not everybody has a clear self-image. As you think about it, you will discover that in some ways you do not see yourself clearly. No doubt you have qualities which you dislike, are ashamed of, or consider disabilities. One of the things you will learn in this book is how to generate new experiences which will reduce the self-hatred.

Why Is Your Self-Image so Important?

It makes the difference between success and failure, happiness and unhappiness, assertion or submissiveness, self-direction or chaos. It

- Tells you how to react to events
- Gives you signals as to whether you are being treated well or ill
- Sets standards for the people you admit into your life
- Helps determine what events are relevant to you
- Gives meaning to events.

Here is an example of how self-image can lead to self-destructive behavior because of self-destructive identification: A woman client of mine started therapy by going out of her way to tell me about all of her bad qualities. She then asked me if she wasn't really a disgusting kind of person. Sometime later, when I observed that she was a chain-smoker, I asked her not to smoke and to tell me how she felt. Her response to my request was "I can't see myself in a healthy way. I get immediate relief from anxiety when I smoke (initial rationalization), and I choose to ignore the long-range consequences." (I commented to her that her knowledge of good hygiene showed that she had some self-protective qualities.) "I indulge myself with cigarettes." (What part of you do you want to kill?) "I expect to die young. It is almost too much to think of myself in a young and healthy way without messing it up. I'm not that good a friend to myself. I'm like a child who fails because her image doesn't allow her to pass."

FROM IDENTIFICATION TO IDENTITY

Identification. As we grow up, many labels are pinned on us by others. Some we give ourselves as a result of how other people treat us. We have a religion, an ethnic name, we are "good" or "bad," we are members of a family, a certain community, "lovable" or "unlovable," "competent" or "incompetent." These old-time out-of-date labels we will call *"identification."* These labels affect our personality.

• We develop a sense of similarity or differences to the people around us.
• We use others' standards as to what is important and valuable. Thus our identification is partly derived from how we experience other people—how they treated us, what they told us about ourselves, and the feelings they stirred up in us.

Identity. As we mature and change, we undergo a creative process. We can experience life and our personality more and more through our own eyes, not those of our parents, teachers, religious mentors, and childhood friends. We have the potential to exchange new values, standards, and goals for the musty and dilapidated ones of our past! This later self-image we will call *"identity."*

DEVELOPING OUR IDENTITY

Identification nuclei are images of ourselves, of real people, of fantasied people whom we expect to nurture or harm us or set standards for us—images which we formed in childhood. Images of ourselves and of important people are organized by our feelings about them. When a mother (or father) takes good care of the child, vague images develop which somehow combine into one or more fantasies, feelings of being loved, an image of the parent, and also of one's self. These images might be composed of both personality qualities and also parts of the body. Comments such as "She has her daddy's personality and her mommy's good looks" can become part of a girl's self-image. When children are *frustrated*, then different kinds of images develop. These are selected and held together by hurt and angry feelings. Such images pose real problems for our adjustment to later life.

What feelings organize our inner world as we grow up? The most important factor is our experience of anger, followed by love. I have suggested elsewhere that the way we experience anger and learn how to deal with it is more important than sex in shaping our personality (Parker, 1972).

Origin of good self-esteem. We form a picture of ourselves, combined with images of other people, all selected by and combined through a common pleasant feeling, e.g., love. This positive or "good" image is the beginning of feelings of self-respect, optimism, and an accepting attitude toward others.

Origin of low self-esteem. We also form other images of ourselves which were stirred up by feelings of being disliked, i.e., when our parents or others were punitive, frustrating, or critical. These nuclei are the beginnings of self-degrading attitudes toward ourselves ("bad' me"), and hating or fearful attitudes toward the world. If the feelings are painful enough, we might separate particular images or parts of them and "project" them into somebody else: We ascribe to others qualities which we possess but which are too hurtful to admit.

Self-hatred. If you are unfortunate enough to have grown up with discouraging experiences, without having developed the resources to experience strength despite them, then your attitude toward life can lead to self-destructiveness. These internal images, together with the picture that you have formed of your own self, create for you a lifelong repetitious script. It is no longer necessary for parents, friends, teachers, ministers, and others to say to us, "You're bad, evil, inadequate, unlovable, incompetent, selfish." We retain the memory of these put-downs and say to these people, "Relax, take it easy. You don't have to work any more criticizing me, because I will do it my-self." The picture we maintain of ourself is degraded; we see ourselves as bad, inadequate, unlovable. Our memory plays a cruel trick on us. It not only retains the image of ourself as unhappy and inadequate, but it also retains the memory of those that did it to us. We then suffer from a kind of auto-intoxi-cation: We keep telling ourselves of all our fatal flaws. The con-sequences include:

- Tolerance for others treating us badly
- Tendency to ruin our projects and relationships
- Great sensitivity to criticism
- Avoiding people for fear of hearing more of the same.

Unfortunately, people seem to cling to these self-destructive habits, which prevents them from relearning how to enjoy their assets and to collaborate with constructive people.

Images of others. We also develop images of other people based upon positive or negative feelings. We form a picture of a "good" mother and a "good" father. We also develop images of a "bad" mother and a "bad" father. All of these images, includ-ing those of ourselves, may have exaggerated or imaginary qualities. They combine experiences occurring at different times. All that they really have in common may be that they were stirred up by pleasant or unpleasant feelings.

After a while, the internal cast of characters becomes even more complicated. We try to imagine what kind of a parent we would really like to have, and we create him or her—an "ideal parent." Then we imagine what kind of a person we would like to be, so that we could get love from the "ideal parent." This becomes our "ego ideal." Then we imagine (in adolescence) what kind of lover we would want to make us feel worthwhile and emotionally fulfilled—and we create Prince or Princess Charming. Moreover, our experiences at times may be so dreadful that particular images develop which are later deeply repressed. They may appear only in dreams or when we are ill or fatigued or under the influence of drugs. Then they bring about high anxiety or terror. These have been called by psychiatrist Harry Stack Sullivan "not me," because ordinarily we are so unaware of them. In reality, they are very much a part of us.

SOME SELF-DESTRUCTIVE PERSONALITIES

Let's see how self-destructive attitudes can spoil one's life.

A man said, "I do everything to avoid success. My father was a competitive parent. It took the form of disparaging my achievements as a child. It led me to an enduring sense of lack of competence relative to my abilities. I was left with anxiety. Moreover, I sabotage myself when success is imminent. I have a real fear of achieving my goals. I purposely fail to properly define my goals and then prevent myself from achieving them. As my awareness has grown, and I have gotten closer to a solution to my problem, my anxiety is increasing. I have a vested interest in self-destruction. My parental imprinting was to remain in the shadow of my father. I have been relatively comfortable in situations where I am not risking anything. I confine myself to unimportant areas. I don't put myself on the line, so I avoid anxiety."

In this man's mind, although he is an adult, his father retains the power he had as a child: ability to punish him, the option of offering or withholding love and other rewards.

A woman offered this experience: "I allow myself to be overwhelmed by believing I can't do what faces me. I have a negative identity and a weak ego. My parents tried to raise a new generation of failures, although it is marvelous to see how my sister has overcome this. One of my goals was to be a good parent. If I could raise my child to be secure I would raise my own security. I lived up to the prophecy of my parents: 'You'll never be successful, because we were never successful.' When my business did achieve success, my parents wouldn't talk to me. I really became successful when I gave up believing what they told me. There had been a need to believe. I was afraid of losing their love. Conditional love is worse than no love. I wasn't willing to buck pressure. If I failed, I was on my own. It was the inevitable act of God. Success to them was good marks, marrying a professional man, in other words, making them look good. Finally, I decided that this was my life. At that time I had no identity. I was my mother's daughter. When I objected to this role, I was told that I was a disgrace for getting divorced. I had to live with them. Think their way or leave. I rebelled by failing after going back to school."

This woman did not see herself as having any particularly valuable qualities of her own. Rather, she was a mother of her daughter, and a mirror image of her parents' self-hatred.

NOT KNOWING WHO YOU ARE

With unclear identity, you will experience a variety of dissatisfactions with your life—specifically, not knowing what you want or how to get it. If you do not have direction in which to express your talents and interests, you will drift or feel that other people are directing your life.

A woman swayed by others' needs. I suggested to her that she "thought of herself as a figment of somebody else's imagination." She replied, "Sometimes when I make love I imagine two other people in erotic situations." Since she felt that others did not understand her, I suggested that in her job and elsewhere she could express her feelings, even if people didn't totally understand. "It is good to know that not everything has to be understood. No matter what I give is never enough. I'm pulled in all directions by different members of my family. My image of myself? I wonder if I exist, feel, and live only in the minds of others, or for myself as well?" During the course of therapy she said, "For the first time I became totally aware, more expressive, and defined. My feelings then became more important than what other people say or think. My own being wasn't so abstract. How little I asked for myself and what I really wanted!" After severe illness she became intensely involved with a creative art form, and said, "I feel egotistic, happy, excited. I have done something fine. I'm moved by it. It's mine."

An intelligent, cultured man submerged by marriage to a demanding woman. While she had helped him to go to college years before, by now he felt that he had repaid his obligation long ago. "I have become a wage earner. There is no time to be anything more than that. I am bent to her will. I am a means to an end." He had lost touch with any unique qualities he experienced.

A man who felt molded by others. I put him into a deep state of relaxation and asked him to create an image of himself. "It was gray clay. I don't know if it was really me. It was covered with clay. It just came out of me. I was sitting here and then saw it." (Do you feel that way?) "Yes and no. You can be clay and let other people mold you or you can be clay and mold yourself. I've let other people do the molding. It didn't have much detail to it. Like a lot of people put their thumbs on it [his image]. I feel under the thumbs of a lot of people. Their marks are there. I don't know if I wanted to make any particular thing out of me. It seems easier to let the world do what it will. It likes to smooth things out, take off the roughness, get rid of the impressions of people that don't seem to fit." (Do people eliminate your uniqueness and originality?) "As a kid you're formed by others." To the writer: "I feel like arguing with you. Should I go through life listening to you all the time?" (My thumb is on you, too. You put me in the same class as those who molded you for selfish reasons.) "Don't you want to help me get free? I don't trust people. I don't want to lose control."

This man was in a difficult emotional situation. He did not see himself as being able to "be himself," but until he could gain more strength he couldn't trust others to offer him a hand with no obligations.

A woman who could use only part of her talents. She felt incompetent in dealing with aspects of her home with which her parents had familiarity. She was successful with areas of her lifestyle which were out of her parents' experience. She completed the back yard of her home and the swimming pool and basement long before she could finish work on the interior. She felt happy about the outside areas. Her parents could not comment on her performance here because they had no experience with a private house.

A woman with no identity as a worker. She had an unsatisfactory work history: "I was not encouraged to follow my career goals. Rather, my parents encouraged me to get a husband. Consequently, I was never serious about anything I did. It was a lark, I was a dilettante. I take jobs that are too easy and not creative." Her identity lacks the image of somebody with something substantial to offer the world.

IDENTITY EXERCISE

The purpose of this exercise is to clarify your sense of identity, i.e., your sense of self-awareness. Specifically, it will help you to see yourself more clearly in those ways in which you feel unique, especially feelings about yourself that have persisted through the years. Clarification of your identity will be extremely important in improving your decision making in such areas as intimate relationships, job performance, and enhancing creativity.

I. Answer the following questions with as many responses as possible. For each answer, state what there is about this particular quality that you like and what you dislike.

A. *"Who am I?"*
B. *"What sort of a person am I?"*
C. *"In what ways am I different from most other people?"*
D. *"In what ways am I like other people?"*
E. *"In what ways has my identity remained constant for many years?"*
F. *"In what ways has my identity changed recently?"*
G. *"What would my identity be like if I were the opposite of the way I am?"* (List the good and bad points if the change were made to the opposite identity.)

II. Take the descriptions of yourself (without the self-accepting and self-disliking statement) and put them in one of the following categories:

Employment: Everything having to do with job and career.

Intimate relations: Everything having to do with your feelings of sexual attractiveness, sexual qualities, emotional needs, feelings, and preferences.

Autonomy: Everything having to do with your ability to use and enjoy your own personality, to be creative, to be self-reliant.

Social: Everything having to do with religious, ethnic, and other groups you see yourself as belonging to; also whether you prefer social participation to actions by yourself.

III. Write a description of

- What you like about your identity
- What you don't like about your identity
- What actions to correct self-dislike you will take.

3) Your Defective Brain

At this point you have probably reached the conclusion that you are self-destructive in some important ways. Wonder why? Grab your seat, because I have bad news for you: *Your brain is defective.*

Why do I offer this depressing information? Self-knowledge can help you to compensate for its deficiencies. Your brain does require careful supervision. On the other hand, it is a very interesting organ. Let me offer an analogy. You are driving on a main highway and you discover that the front end of your car is out of alignment. When you apply the brakes the car drifts to the left into oncoming traffic. Deciding to head for the nearest garage, you compensate by steering a bit in the opposite direction.

Does it come to you as a surprise that the chief cause of self-destructiveness is the gross inefficiency of the human brain? No wonder. You have been taught that the brain is a marvel of complexity, its billions of cells serving such functions as rational thought, emotion, coordination, and perception. Only its basic deficiencies help to account for such realities of life as the slaughter of tens of millions of people, the emotional brutality which is so common, the failure of so many marriages, the high proportion of neurotics, the inability of society to solve educational and employment problems, the frequency of suicide.

If you are to avoid self-destructiveness, you will have to admit that your brain is not the reliable computer you'd like it to be. For example:

- You frequently don't see the world accurately
- Your self-understanding is often weak
- Your feelings are not always to be trusted
- You don't fully understand the relationships you have with important people
- You don't remember what it is convenient for you to forget
- You remember lots of events in ways that never happened.

To avoid self-destructiveness you will have to understand the realities and limitations of how the mind works. You will then be able to undo many misconceptions, remembered injuries, and fallacious ideologies that you were taught or maybe invented yourself. Of course, this makes up the distasteful topic of self-discipline.

You may be asking a sensible question: Are you not exaggerating? No. I mean every word that I have written. Nevertheless you may persist: Are there not worthy and even notable achievements of the human brain? Of course. Some of my happiest moments—shared by thousands of others—were listening to performances of Beethoven, Schubert, Brahms, Mahler, and Mozart performed by Bruno Walter and the virtuoso musicians of the New York Philharmonic. The sculptures of Michelangelo, the paintings of Rembrandt, the formulations of Einstein, the plays of Shakespeare, Milton's poetry, and the pioneering courage and imagination of Freud are all examples of the brain integrating and producing products of universal value. Why then do I insist that the human brain is inefficient and the cause of self-destructiveness? Because its functioning in the emotional area is a joke. (However, as Philip Roth's Portnoy commented, "It's a joke that I am living personally.") Let me be specific as to why the brain can be considered to be poorly designed.

1. Its basic design may have been fixed about 100,000 years ago with no later modifications that we know of.

2. When change has occurred, new parts have been added without disconnecting or eliminating old ones.

3. Each half (cerebral hemisphere) copes with and remembers somewhat different kinds of information and, generally, is not on talking terms with the other half.

4. The brain offers toward the solution of current problems

out-of-date information that is spoiled and smelly and should have been thrown out years ago.

5. Sexual preferences, and perhaps other basic attitudes, seem at least partly determined (in some of us, at least) by the delicate balance and intricate scheduling of secretions of sexual and other hormones while we are still in the womb.

Because I don't expect you to take such subversive attitudes toward your personal brain on faith, here is a review of your head by some outstanding authorities:

Berta Scharrer, in the 47th James Arthur Lecture (on the evolution of the human brain), sponsored by the American Museum of Natural History (1977), asserts that important regulating neurohormones (peptides) related to the by-now well-known brain opiates that affect pain and mood can be traced back to worms, insects, snails, and slugs.

Candace Pert (1974), a leading neurophysiologist, shows that tiny brain structures (opiate binding sites, or action sites for neurohormones) are found in the lowly slime hags (jawless fishes) and in all mammals. In fact, there is a constancy of structures designed to receive particular neurohormones in the limbic system, a primitive region of the brain involved with emotion. The limbic system, in turn, evolved from the important smell-brain (olfactory lobes) and other structures of primitive fish and sharks. Gray matter and newer structures are just connected in. We will see the great importance of these neurohormones to our emotional life in the next chapter.

Gaither and Stein (1979), writing in the journal Science, point out the similarities between the ways that reptiles and mammals organize information from the world in related parts of the brain. The similarities, they say, represent an anatomical plan "that was retained during the evolution to mammalian forms more than 180 million years ago."

David Crews (1979), in an article in Scientific American, states that important hormonal influences on sexual behavior are found both in lizards and mammals, from which he infers that this effect "is ancient in evolutionary terms."

This evidence that brain structure and functioning are ancient is only a hint of what will be revealed by future research. We will learn more and more about how our reactions are shaped and restrained by the workings of our brain, glands, and other vital organs. How is it of concern to all of us? It should lead us to find out what are our most comfortable styles of reacting so that we can achieve reasonable goals with minimal cost and built-in resistance to inappropriate styles of action. In addition, since many of you are now seeking or will at some time seek professional psychotherapeutic or counseling assistance, it should alert you to psychotherapists who may mislead you as to your potential or real nature because of their grandiosity or ignorance of the facts of life. More about this in Chapter 20.

I have already made the point that brain design doesn't seem to have changed for perhaps 100,000 years. Some of your difficulties undoubtedly arise from the fact that your brain evolved from your ancestors' struggle to exist and procreate in a world that was vastly different from today's. (See Parker, *Effective Decisions and Emotional Fulfillment*, Chapter 6; Nancy Tanner and Zihlman, 1976; Zihlman and Tanner, 1978; Zihlman, 1978a, b). Please follow this line of reasoning. It appears that about 3 million years ago the human (hominid) line was separated from the line leading to the great apes (Isaac, 1978; Washburn, 1979). Although our ancestors' brain was no larger than that of some of our hairy cousins, maybe a pound compared to the two to three pounds of today's human brain, it probably was organized little differently. There was one form of behavior which made your remote ancestors different from other lines of primates, and which was selected by the workings of heredity to be passed along by heredity: the capacity to share food in the social group (Tanner and Zihlman, 1976; Zihlman, 1978a; Zihlman and Tanner, 1978).

This speculation concerning primitive social structure has some contemporary relevance. At one time it was emphasized that man was the Great Hunter, and woman the Primeval Mother. Well, it was true, sort of. The only problem is that when you are a primitive, hunting big game is pretty hard. I remember an anthropological film that showed bushmen trailing such a passive beast as a giraffe for days, losing track of it, being able to wound it but not easily bringing it down, etc., until the unfortunate animal died of shock. Such an expenditure of time and energy seems grossly uneconomical. During such times, the women would be gathering fruits, lizards, and nuts, which might have been the mainstay of the diet (Kolata, 1975). Does it come as a surprise to you that women are more important to human survival than men? It shouldn't. Ask the nearest mother!

Anyway, "food, feeding behavior, and associated traits seem to provide the best explanation of the evolutionary facts, just as they do for almost all animal groups," according to anthropologist David Pilbeam (1978). Apparently, many of the adaptations made to earlier conditions that shaped human nature are grossly irrelevant to contemporary life.

To understand why we deal so poorly with our world, one must understand that our brains evolved over a long period of time, in conjunction with changes of posture, muscles, glands, and other organs. Then—say 100,000 years ago—the complexity and difficulty of life began to accelerate. Consider this timetable:

- 3,000,000 years ago: hominids bid goodbye to the apes
- 2,000,000 years ago: first tools created (Isaac, 1978)
- 1,500,000 years ago: first rock carvings and paintings (Arbman, 1964)
- 100,000 years ago: design for brain accepted and put into production
- 60,000 years ago: first flowers found in graves (Solecki, 1975)
- 45,000–35,000 years ago: modern man appeared (Klein, 1974); language evolved (Washburn and Harding, 1975)
- 40,000 years ago: first use of fire
- 13,000 years ago: grain was ground
- 10,000 years ago: last ice age ended (Klein, 1974)
- 9,500 years ago: first complicated settlement (Moore, 1979)
- 7,000 years ago; early switch from hunting and gathering to agriculture (Moore, 1979)
- 5,500 years ago: the Old Kingdom of Egypt.

Events are moving too fast for our poor brains to catch up! As Dr. Adrienne Zihlman summed it up in 1978 (reference b): "The events of about the past 10,000 years, since agriculture began, have had a negligible effect on the human brain and body that originated on the African Savanna and evolved over several million years." Things have happened too fast. Yet, many of the qualities bred into our genes in earlier times are irrelevant for most of us today. In a fascinating article by C. D. Darlington in *Natural History* (May 1970), he notes that many of our ancestors were either farmers who domesticated crops or pastoralists who cultivated animals. The farmer's life "depended on his prudence and industry in handling the soil and crops. . . . [Farmers] are inbred, conservative, and traditional, stubborn but peaceful. How different is the pastoralist! He is correspondingly attached to his animals, but his animals can move and usually have to move in search of pasture. He is therefore mobile, alert, and aggressive. He will steal the cattle and the women of his neighbors. Consequently, he is relatively outbred." Moreover, our forebears were also *selected by the species they cultivated*, since only those with the wit and qualities to take advantage of the crops or animals they used would prosper.

While food-raising differences were only a fraction of the factors that shaped our genetic heritage, they fostered mental and physical qualities necessary for survival too few generations ago to have been since "unbred." These attributes, among others, are only partially relevant to modern living. Julian Huxley (1958) pointed out that cultural evolution proceeds at a rate hundreds of times that of biological evolution. In any population there is a variety of genetic qualities. This ensures that some will survive as circumstances change. Therefore, many individuals have characteristics unsuited to the particular environment in which they live. A pioneer in community mental health, William Healy (1959), concluded that it is a "curious anomaly . . . when, in a given situation, such as that of restricted city life, great strength and activity is a liability for socialized conduct output, rather than an asset."

OUR BIOLOGICAL HERITAGE

Because the nervous system did not develop in a fully coordinated fashion, our emotions and rational processes are poorly integrated with each other. Some structures remain relatively unchanged from their state of development in primitive creatures; others were added in the course of evolution. The core of the brain, similar in structure and function to that of the early vertebrates, not only exercises control over functions like nutrition, breathing, and elimination, but also modifies such emotional reactions as anger, fear, and sex. This "limbic system" exchanges influence with the cerebral covering (cortex) which is responsible for perceiving the world, learning, movement, etc. The consequence is that our lives are a mixture of fact, fantasy, and physiological functioning to a degree that we are frequently ignorant.

The brain confuses time. After stress, the body continues to react for a long period of time. For example, according to *Executive Fitness Newsletter* (January 26, 1980, p. 4), a graduate student found that his heartbeat increased to 150 per minute when he began his doctoral examination, and did not return to the normal rate of 72 per minute until hours later. It has been claimed by Brady (1962) that such physiological reactions can continue for up to seventy-two hours. Widespread physiological effects persist after significant events for a long interval. It is not surprising, then, that subsequent unrelated events become associated with the unpleasant feelings stimulated by something that happened hours before. Anxiety, terror, guilt, bodily reactions, ideas, and events thus become unified experiences.

Moreover, the brain remembers in a distorted way the events of childhood. This is a serious defect, since children think and feel differently than adults. They organize and combine events, fantasies, and feelings in distinctive ways. According to Jean Piaget and Barbel Inhelder (Hall, ed., 1970), the child considers his own point of view as the only possible one; and the memory code (the language in which we remember) changes with the years. This is why we have difficulty remembering our childhood. As we grow up, images of ourselves, our parents, and the rest of the world become strongly connected with feelings. Our images, fantasies, and concepts formed in childhood consist of patterns and parts vastly different from those we would develop and organize as adults. For example, such patterns may consist of bodily feelings (pleasant or unpleasant) intertwined with an image of some aspect of ourselves and some aspect of our parents.

These *identification nuclei* influence our experiences and reactions for a long time. *But they are very hard to put into the language we use as adults.* A mother's anger or a father's criticism of a child as a "bad boy or girl," followed by a spanking and supperless banishment upstairs to a dark room, in a state of anxiety, rage, loneliness, hunger, reduced self-esteem, and hopelessness, create a condition which can haunt a child forever. These moods and memories come back in times of dreams and nightmares, fear, hallucinogenic drug use, illness, emotional stress, sickness, rejection, fatigue, aloneness, and darkness. Our defective brain stores such experiences for future reference; thus they influence behavior years after they have become irrelevant. For example, a chronic feeling of inferiority affects school, employment, choice of friends, sexual relationships, creativity, and other aspects of life.

The emotionally brutalized boy can go to his room and develop a fantasy like this: "When I am older, I am really going to be strong. No woman is going to push me around like that. *I am going to get even.* You wait and see." This could be the identification nucleus of a domineering, sadistic man who learned from his childhood suffering to feel vengeance, not compassion. He is the child abuser, wife beater, rapist, the overbearing brute who serves as an active link in the world's chain of suffering—to act out his childhood fantasy of becoming strong, long after he has reached strength and independence. The brain a magnificent organ, indeed!

Here is an example of persistent childhood fearfulness: A man said, "I am a very good trumpet player. Once I walked into a bar where a kid was playing. I borrowed the instrument and played well. I thought to myself, I'm giving him a lesson. Suddenly the blood rushed from my head. I thought I would faint. I handed him back the instrument, ran away, and didn't recover until I had gone two blocks. I thought of my father giving me a lesson. He thought he could sing. He ridiculed my mother for singing out of tune and ridiculed me when I started to play. This memory comes back to me when I think I have an effect on my audience. When I see musicians with smiles on their faces I get nervous and stop. Panic sets in because I think I'm in my father's place giving a lesson! I'm dominant and your opinion is shit! I displace him and think, Get out of the house. We'll reverse roles. I remember meeting a top trumpet player who complimented me. I said to him, 'I stunk.' He got angry: 'I know what I can hear.' "

This unhappy man's experience illustrates some of the ways in which our brain is defective:

- Old events are still disorganizing.
- Self-esteem doesn't replace self-contempt.
- Physiological reactions occur as though there were mortal danger.
- We play different roles than our own and are not even aware of it until too late.
- Trivial similarities between current people in our lives and old-time significant persons cause us to transfer outdated reactions to present situations.
- New experiences which would give us greater effectiveness are avoided.

The unconscious. A reasonable definition of the unconscious is the presence of significant effects of forgotten experiences, of which we are not aware. If your unconscious processes were to be described, they would involve images, deep feelings, ideas, and details of people and experiences linked together according to the similarity of the feelings they aroused, or accidental occurrences at the same time, without any logical order or connection. Such unconscious images, or "complexes," to use Carl Jung's term, remain active over long periods of life. They may become more virulent rather than fading away. You may ask, How can such distortions remain despite the corrective effects of forgetting, logic, and new experiences? The answer lies in your defective brain.

It appears that the right hemisphere of the brain develops before the left (Bakan, 1977–78). Thus, our early life is recorded by structures which are primarily responsible for regulating emotional processes (Schwartz, Davidson, and Mayr, 1975) and images (Bakan, 1977–78). However, in Western culture words and logic are generally more highly valued by the educated classes (such as the reader of this book). In the majority (right-handed people), these functions are primarily controlled by the left side of the brain. Access to feelings and information stored on the right is restricted, either by lack of a common language with the left brain, or by active inhibition of transmission during waking hours. However, at night the censor is asleep, and when we dream, we experience the contents of our unconscious, including fantasies, repressed feelings, and conflicts. In short, we inhibit those mental functions which are related to our unconscious.

This ability of the brain to suppress painful information has a paradoxical effect. Some hurtful feelings (forgotten perfectly) are not permanently eliminated, and may continue to trouble us. Moreover, new impulses that are associated with guilt or the expectation of punishment (neurotic anxiety) are also repressed, hidden from awareness. For example, to prevent ourselves from yielding to feelings and actions punishable by a smack or no TV for a week, our brain pretended after we were punished that such healthy thoughts as sex and anger don't exist. However, punished attitudes do show themselves indirectly, without our being aware of either our own motives or their effect on others. Many a seductive person would be outraged by the accusation of being a tease. The most outrageous acts of aggression are denied and some excuse offered in justification.

Unconscious motives. There are many ways of seeing the world and reacting that "protect" us through self-delusion. We kid ourselves that we are good little boys and girls, obedient to our parents, religious leaders, teachers, and others who have a vested interest in our behavior and morality. In reality we may project, that is, attribute our hostile wishes to another person, then attack or abuse him without realizing we are the creator of the hatred actions. We may displace our feelings, as, for example, to make ourselves feel better when our employer picks on us, we spank the kid, yell at our spouse, or kick the dog. There are other forms of self-delusion. An obsession is an idea that runs through the mind which is related to a forbidden wish, but is disguised so that we are unaware of it. A compulsion is a repetitive action that shows symbolically what we would like to do but are afraid to carry out. A hysterical conversion reaction is a reduced ability to perceive the world or to do something (blindness, deafness, paralysis) that has been forbidden, and prevents us from seeing or doing what would displease Mommy.

If you are not yet convinced that your brain is defective, that itself might be proof that it is!

What Would an Effective Brain Be Like?

Such a useful organ would

- Live in the present
- Present us with an accurate account of the past
- Erase out-of-date information
- Learn with new experiences
- Prevent us from getting involved with extraneous issues
- Understand genuine dangers and keep us away from them
- Not create false dangers which restrict our lives.

WHAT TO DO?

Recognize the various ways in which your beliefs, attitudes, values, and identity mislead you. In this way, you will be able to unlearn defeatism and self-destructive habits which would have been avoided by a better-designed brain. No, don't ask for a brain transplant. Nobody has a better brain than you. They all need a little adjustment. Read on!

4) Your Childish Values and Beliefs

Let's look at your values and beliefs. Do you think of yourself as an adult? Well, if we look closely at the way you think, I'm afraid that many of your ideas were developed when you were a lovable kid but not too perceptive. Certainly not the bold and independent thinker you are today. In this chapter I will alert you to the importance of thinking about your values and beliefs and then determining whether they lead you to constructive or self-destructive actions.

An excellent summary of how belief and value systems work was offered by psychiatrist Jerome D. Frank (1977): "To select from and make sense of the welter of their experience, humans need a moral and cognitive map of the universe. Such maps may be termed *belief systems*, and they include beliefs as to the nature of reality and of causality, the nature of knowledge, and codes of ethics—that is, descriptions of valued and disvalued behaviors. Ultimately, all belief systems rest on value premises that for the believer are not open to question and that cannot be disproved by appeal to experience. . . . They are articles of faith." The map supplied by a belief system provides a guide *as to what choices we have for action*, and *what to pay attention to* out of all the events and feelings we experience. Furthermore, it binds together people with similar beliefs. Sometimes our beliefs justify any kind of mistreatment of outsiders. Finally, beliefs serve to relieve anxiety by linking our existence as individuals to some permanent value such as faith in the Eternal.

Beliefs are taught to us when we begin life weak and vulnerable. Receiving affection and approval may be conditional upon the parents or other adults getting particular responses they crave. The child must be "nice," or obedient, or active, or quiet, and so forth. Your attitudes toward cleanliness, scholastic attainment, professional status, politics, sex, and showing your anger have probably been conditioned by parents who were good and affectionate to you only when you performed on cue, whether on the potty or the piano. Any deviation from explicitly stated parental values or, worse yet, their *hidden* beliefs was threatened with the loss of love, spanking, banishment, scorn, turned backs, or other examples of parental tenderness and competence. You aren't convinced? Bring home a homosexual partner or someone of a different race or religion, or file for divorce. You may learn that your devoted parents are devoted primarily to their own social anxieties, prejudices, drives to power, or need for family and neighbors' approval.

THE PRESSURE TOWARD CONFORMITY

What did your parents need from you? They needed a child of whom they could be proud. Therefore, your growing mind had to be molded to this end. How? By meeting your parents' fantasies of how a certain kind of child would make them look good in the eyes of their family, friends, and community. He can be molded toward *conformity* by being punished physically, isolated, scorned, threatened with hell, compared with more acquiescent peers, by being nagged, having other siblings treated as favorites, being disliked and suffering other forms of nastiness and abuse—all this in the name of providing pride and pleasure for his parents. However, if the child expresses the idea that his parents are ridiculous, unfeeling, excessively demanding, selfish, unmindful of his needs, or plain spoilsports, he risks being considered "bad," rebellious, naughty, dirty, sinful, immoral, or some other degrading thing.

Your parents want you to be a carbon copy not of their own behavior but of their cherished fantasies, ideals, fanaticisms, and prejudices. These were learned from their parents, teachers, clergy, political leaders, soap-opera writers, fictional heroes or heroines, media advertising directors, and other emotionally inadequate or inappropriate molders of values. The values that were implanted in you may have had their origins thousands of years ago in prehistory, or some other country, or in the tortured mind of an emotionally disturbed or hating person, perhaps a cynical producer of TV pulp dramas or an ignorant, prejudiced cult leader. However, those values are now yours to shape your loves, your goals, your attitudes toward employment and creativity, toward friends and associates, toward politics, civil affairs, neighbors, and military service. Oh yes, they are also yours to influence the way you treat your children, evaluate your employees, relate to your dates or mate, select your neighbors, vote, choose entertainment, decorate your house, select your clothing, pick courses and career, and spend your leisure time.

A Value Checklist for Dating

Has your partner the right height, hair color, education, occupation, social background, personality, sexual attitude, preference for entertainment, attitude toward marriage, children, and neighborhood? Does he/she vote for the right party, have the right attitudes toward war, radicals, welfare, crime in the streets, left-wingers, right-wingers?

Politics. People rarely decide in advance where their real best interest lies, and then vote or try to influence their representatives or other voters in a sensible (by their own standards) way. In the area of government, foreign relations, and war, old-time values and experiences are cheerfully transferred as solutions to today's dangerous realities. It would not take much investigation to detect similarities between a person's political values, belief as to what to expect of authority, accepting violence as a solution and his early experiences of authority and how angry feelings were handled within the family (see below for descriptions of various types of families).

The next time you cast your vote, start a political struggle, or propose making a military assault upon a supposed enemy, ask yourself, Am I intelligent, well-informed, rational, well-meaning, or am I an angry, frustrated, incompetent person continuing the old family fight? Then I suggest that you ask yourself carefully, Is this point of view in my own best interest today or tomorrow? Is this amount of violence (or passivity) necessary or realistic? How many innocent people will be hurt if the government really does what I want? Is that group out there just as malevolent as I imagine them to be (like the _____ when I was a kid)? If the answer is yes, you are probably acting out neurotic feelings of injustice and rage emanating from unkindness to you in your childhood and are engaged in transferring your anger to somebody else.

Religion. How about destructive religious values? I know one person whose priest yelled at him in the privacy of the confessional, within earshot of others, that if he continued to masturbate he would become insane. Please don't accuse me of being anti-Catholic. Some Orthodox Jewish families have the pleasant custom of the mother slapping her daughter on the inception of menstruation. Their men believe that women should be isolated in a separate part of the synagogue and not be approached during menstruation or even afterward until they have had a ceremonial bath—as if Jewish mamas didn't keep themselves and anything under their control as aseptic as an operating room. The Protestants are not always accepting of little derelictions either. I remember trying to take the director of religious education of a Protestant church to a nice restaurant in the vicinity of the pitiful little town in which we both worked. She refused even to enter because adjacent to the dining room was a bar, and she was teaching the children in her care not to drink. Result: We went to a local greasy spoon. Subsequently she married a local man with a drinking problem (like her father) who beat her up.

Role. Another area in which the child is frequently assaulted is in being trained to assume a particular sexual or social role. If he is a male, then he must be dominant, emotionally unresponsive, and sexually assertive (assuming that he isn't impotent from fear of insanity, hairy palms, hell, castration, or having his hands burned). He is taught by his mates to "score" and by his sexually frustrated mother to treat women like the Virgin Mary. His school insists that he conform in dress, deportment, and grades, while his peers want him to play, to fight, and to resist the feminizing atmosphere of the school. His parents want him to keep up with the Joneses, restraining his needs, but they can't be bothered either to explain the genuine values and costs of conformity or to tell the Joneses to shove it.

If you are a girl, from the beginning you were given a doll, a baby carriage, and a toy stove that could electrocute you if you touched it with wet hands. In school did you go to shop or to cooking classes? Unless you were raised in a really healthy sexual environment you were taught that the genital area must be held more inviolate than Fort Knox. That's not the end of the story. Your mother then either sent you powdered and lipsticked on dates before you could spell sanitary napkin, or kept you locked up after seven-thirty for fear that some genital stimulation would ruin you worse than the Wreck of the Hesperus. Now, daughter, remember this: No man will respect you if you let him touch you, and I won't respect you if you are not married at eighteen.

THE EFFECT OF HAND-ME-DOWN VALUES

We can no more succeed in life with hand-me-down values than we can wear any piece of clothing somebody offers us. Childhood values may simply not fit our current identity and lifestyle, and if they do, we may find that they are out of fashion. This is the "generation gap." Although there is never complete agreement within a community concerning what attitudes to take, there is often some consensus. Conformists know what is expected of them. Brave, reckless, or rebellious people know what is expected of them, and what the costs of deviation are. What happens, however, if you learned to conform to certain ideas, and then with the passage of time the consensus within your community changes? Perhaps your children's ideals are repugnant to yours, or you cannot stand your parents' ideals. Maybe you assumed that you and your spouse were in agreement, only to find that after a period of time you can't stand the sight of each other because the values/rewards/dislikes in your lives are opposed. A frequent problem is that experienced by the person who marries while having the sexual standards of one generation, and is subsequently divorced, separated, or widowed, only to find himself/herself as a single person in a community of other single people with vastly different values and attitudes (Parker, *Living Single Successfully*).

Values are often very hard to change. Why? Sometimes our values are not clear, or they were taught to us by people whose support is important. Now we can understand why values can be so influential even though we may not be aware of how they shape our feelings and decisions. They start to form at so early an age that their origin can be forgotten, or they can be repressed along with painful childhood experiences. Pressure to conform can be direct, or it can take the subtle form of lack of rewards or acceptance by our associates. We then achieve, if not great satisfaction, at least the reward of staying out of trouble. Unfortunately, the cost of rebelling is frequently very high. One may find himself outside society, or in its lower depths, if one insists that a private or minority set of values is superior to that of the Establishment.

Lack of self-understanding. Here is an instance of a woman who was very troubled because she did not understand her values very clearly: "I'm really floundering. I read that we derive our goals from our essential values. You go back to the values which were handed down to you as a child. I think back and I can't remember my parents telling me anything. I am bereft of values. They were fine outstanding people. I didn't get any admonishments, but I didn't get anything else either. I was reaching for something to start from, and then I could say I reject that. There weren't even any of the stereotyped values or any flag-waving. Little values, yes, like pledge allegiance to the flag and honesty is the best policy. How can I choose a goal? I was trying to grasp something and I can't. *I feel like a wasted human resource.*"

Sometimes it is better to have some form of guidance to use as a standard (and perhaps against which to rebel) than to enter mature life floundering.

Confusion caused by lack of clear values. A construction worker realized that he was in the wrong career, since his true values were education, art, and human relations. Another man, an artist whose chief love was fine art, realized that his disappointment in his work had been because he overidealized business matters (e.g., commercial art and packaging).

SCALE OF VALUES

I have devised the following Scale of Values in order to help you understand your own value system and those of the important people in your life. It is based upon the comments that many people have made at my workshops and in my psychotherapeutic practice, my study of employment, and reading about social conditions. It has been useful in career and personal counseling. The instructions and scoring sheet follow:

I. Temperamental Values
(Nonverbal expression of energy and emotion)

1. *Commitment vs. Unrestraint.* Some people enjoy the idea of responsibility and the knowledge that other people are relying upon them. They feel that they have mobilized their energies toward some goal or purpose. Others want mobility, freedom, and the opportunity to change their plans according to their own pleasure.

2. *Struggle/Excitement vs. Peace/Calm.* For some, the idea of using their energy, strength, and mind makes life worthwhile, is important, and gives a sense of vitality or accomplishment. For others, peace of mind and calmness are important, and their decisions are designed to bring this about.

3. *Risk vs. Security.* Some enjoy engaging in activities with high stakes and an uncertain outcome. Taking risks can be prestigious in your eyes or your colleagues'. Others prefer to devote themselves to tasks in which the outcome is more predictable even if the gains are smaller.

II. Philosophical Values
(Meaning of life)

4. *Grandeur vs. Simplicity.* Are you elevated by observing or participating in events which are impressive, lofty, and complex, such as ceremonies; or do you prefer to be stirred by situations which are unadorned, natural, unpretentious, and plain?

5. *Religion/Spirituality vs. Naturalism/Unreligiosity.* Many people are influenced by faith, intuition, mysticism, and other nonmaterial abstract ideas. Others seek hard facts, personal observation, and scientific principles to explain the meaning of life and provide guidance in making decisions.

6. *Future Goals vs. Present Pleasures/Play.* Some people plan toward future benefits rather than immediate gain. They work for distant objectives. Others want to enjoy life in the present and don't want to put off immediate pleasure.

III. Authority Values
(Beliefs concerning organizations/leaders)

7. *Conformity vs. Rebelliousness.* For some, the wisest choice is to agree with the values/decisions of a family, organization, or community, since it reduces conflicts, gains support, and ultimately increases security and emotional fulfillment. Opposed is the attitude that submitting to authority is emotionally wrong, stunts one's growth, and yields conditions damaging to one's well-being.

8. *Leadership vs. Self-reliance.* One's well-being is served by having confidence in strong individuals (not organizations, as in 7) to provide guidance, support, safety, and happiness. In contrast, one is intelligent and competent enough to function effectively alone without looking to a stronger personality for leadership.

9. *Autocratic vs. Individualistic.* Leaders should have the power to limit the freedom of individuals in order to achieve the greatest good for the most people vs. the idea that individuals can judge their own benefit more than self-appointed, appointed, or elected leaders.

IV. Materialism
(Creating something of value)

10. *Economic.* Money and what it buys are measures of personal value. Goods, services, and lifestyle purchasable by money are of high importance. Money also brings status and security.

11. *Achievement and Career.* A successful career and professional accomplishments are worthwhile to the point of sacrificing pleasures and obligations toward family, friends, and community.

12. *Social Utility and Pragmatism.* Employment, hobbies, and other activities have to be of some value to oneself or to society.

V. Human Relations
(The importance of relationships with particular people)

13. *Family.* The well-being and unity of the family is the primary consideration in guiding one's decisions.

14. *Personal Relationships.* To have friends and be close to

people is more important than other considerations. Life is empty without contact and support.

15. *Being Liked.* The approval of others is an important source of value and well-being, even to the point of holding back opinions or feelings for fear of creating antagonism or unnecessary strife.

VI. Humanism
(Welfare of society)

16. *Altruism.* One should sacrifice one's personal welfare for the benefit of others, e.g., through professional work, religious obligations, charity, and donations.

17. *Honesty.* Dealing fairly and openly with people is the biggest value, as opposed to using guile and taking hidden advantage to maximize one's own welfare.

18. *Respect.* There is something special about human life and the rights of individuals, even to the point of disapproving of the death penalty for murderers.

VII. Status
(Personal values that come from high standing in the community)

19. *Power.* It is important to be influential, give orders, determine the course of events, and to exercise power, even though one's part in it is not known.

20. *Prestige and Recognition.* Fame, acclaim, and honor are important, and can be achieved through professional work, political action, humanitarian acts, as well as military, social, artistic, and athletic activities.

21. *Social Standing.* It is important to be a member of the elite, e.g., by virtue of birth, family, clubs, organizations, the right company. Social standing comes from being accepted by the right group, rather than personal achievement as in 20.

VIII. Autonomy
(Enjoyment of one's personality)

22. *Creativity.* Bringing something into the world as its maker, perhaps a totally new achievement or simply a familiar product made by one personally.

23. *Culture and Aesthetics.* Devotion to the arts, which makes

one feel in contact with timeless or universal experiences, can overcome differences between people over time and culture.

24. *Learning.* It is good to belong to the community of scholars and have love for knowledge and philosophy as sources of information about universal values, guides for understanding of the world, and for their own sake.

INSTRUCTIONS: PARKER SCALE OF VALUES

Values may be defined as attitudes toward life which guide our actions. We are attracted or repelled by certain events, circumstances, activities, and feelings. As a consequence, goals which are attractive to some people are repugnant or undesirable to others. People differ considerably in their values. Self-understanding in this area is extremely important in making prudent decisions with regard to career, personal relationships, and handling money. *All scores should reflect the way you act and feel, not the way you would like to be.*

The Scale of Values is divided into Parts I and II. (Use page 40 as your worksheet.) The instructions for each part are different.

Part I

A. This section covers the first three subsections (I, II, III), each of which has three pairs of Values. These pairs represent opposite poles, i.e., opposing attitudes toward certain common values.

B. Each of the three subsections in Part I is scored separately (paragraphs 1–3, 4–6, 7–9). For each part, pick the one Value which seems most important to you and mark it "1." Then, put an "X" on the side of the page opposite it so that the alternate aspect of this Value is eliminated. For example, if you feel that "Commitment" is your highest Value in the "Temperamental Values" subsection, then you would mark it "1" and you would place an "X" at "Unrestraint," since you cannot value both of these simultaneously according to their description. Then, determine which of the remaining Temperamental Values are most important to you, and on the score sheet, mark it "2." Place an "X" opposite it on the page. Finally, for the remaining pair, mark one side "3" and the remaining item "X."

SCALE OF VALUES
Scoring Sheet

Part I

I. TEMPERAMENT
(Conflict)

1. Commitment	( )	____ ( )	Unrestraint
2. Struggle/Excitement	( )	____ ( )	Peace/Calm
3. Risk	( )	____ ( )	Security

II. PHILOSOPHICAL

4. Grandeur	( )	____ ( )	Simplicity
5. Religion/Spiritual	( )	____ ( )	Naturalism/Unreligiosity
6. Future Goals	( )	____ ( )	Present Pleasures

III. AUTHORITY

7. Conformity	( )	____ ( )	Rebelliousness
8. Leadership	( )	____ ( )	Self-Reliance
9. Autocratic	( )	____ ( )	Individualistic

Part II

IV. MATERIALISM
10. Economic ____
11. Achievement ____
12. Social Utility ____ Sum ____

V. HUMAN RELATIONS
13. Family ____
14. Personal Relations ____
15. Being Liked ____ Sum ____

VI. HUMANISM
16. Altruism ____
17. Honesty ____
18. Respect ____ Sum ____

VII. STATUS
19. Power ____
20. Prestige/Recognition ____
21. Social Standing ____ Sum ____

VIII. AUTONOMY
22. Creativity ____
23. Culture/Aesthetics ____
24. Learning ____ Sum ____

C. In the same way, score the remaining two sections of Part I. You will have three sets of Values rated, "1," "2," and "3."

D. In every set, you *may* have doubt as to which side of a pair of Values is most important to you. If you are not sure as to your preference for one side or another of a pair, you can mark "C" in the middle. This means that you are in conflict between these two values. Avoid the use of "C" if possible.

Part II

E. Each of the fifteen Values of Part II (paragraphs 10–24) is to be ranked in order of most valuable ("1") to least valuable or most disliked ("15").

F. One easy way of performing this task is as follows: Read the fifteen descriptions. Choose the Value which is most significant to you (positive). Mark the blank space as "1." Then select the Value which is least important or most distasteful. Mark it as "15." Then select the remaining most important Value and mark it as "2." The remaining least important value is marked "14," and so on.

G. Add up the three sets of scores and place them in the blanks marked "Sum" on the scoring sheet.

H. The lowest sum of scores represents your highest value in this section, and the highest score the area of values least important to you.

5) Understanding Your Emotional Life

In this chapter we will continue the process of self-understanding based upon current scientific information, not the unsavory blend of speculation and idealized goals which too often are foisted upon the public. There are real functions of the brain which place limitations upon your moods, shape your behavior, and make it troublesome for you to achieve your goals. The task of scientific description of human nature has only begun, but there is enough information to help you to understand yourself. The key points to be made in this chapter are:

• Some of your emotional reactions are not under your conscious control.

• Feelings and emotions were originally built into your nervous system to serve physical survival.

• Your emotional life is shaped by long-lived biological qualities called temperament, which make certain kinds of reactions more comfortable than others.

• There are genuine inborn differences between people in their emotional reactions.

The French philosopher René Descartes evolved his system around the idea that "I think, therefore I am." The writer trusts that those who concern themselves with these matters will not judge him too harshly if he offers a modest proposal: Conviction of our existence comes as firmly from our feelings as from our thoughts. Therefore, with considerable trepidation, I am offering a slight wrinkle for the body of philosophic thought. I modify René's idea to read, "I feel, therefore I am!"

I believe that our feelings are the most significant aspects of life. They are the substance of pleasure and pain. Some people even complain about the lack of feelings in their life, i.e., that their emotions are "shades of gray." Although individuals come into psychotherapy with a variety of goals and complaints, I think that their real request is "Doctor, I want to *feel* better."

Feelings give us a variety of both *information* and *misinformation.* Feelings are not only of importance by themselves. They offer information to you as to your reaction to your world, and how the world is treating you. It is to be hoped you are aware of your feelings, interpret them correctly, are not misled by feelings which come from the past, and react to your real interests and not what other people tell you is important for you.

ADAPTATION

Adaptation is the way in which we fit into our world or "niche," i.e., cope with reality. It means the techniques that we use to get along with people, to be successful, enjoy life, and above all, the ways in which our personality changed as we grew up and moved into new situations. When our usual adaptation doesn't work, we get upset and uncomfortable, and are *maladapted.* When we *adapt* to our niche successfully, we are happy, productive, and have rewarding relationships with other people.

Some Categories of Adaptive Behavior

The following breakdown of kinds of behavior which are part of your emotional life was prepared by Robert Plutchik (1980) in his exploration of what organisms *must do to survive.*

- *Protection*—avoiding danger or harm
- *Destruction*—eliminating barriers to satisfaction of your needs
- *Incorporation*—accepting good things from the world, like sex, food, and friends
- *Rejection*—expelling something harmful, whether it is food or destructive people
- *Reproduction*—sexual contact
- *Reintegration*—putting our lives together when somebody who has been nurturant has gone

- *Orientation*—becoming familiar with strange or unfamiliar stimuli or situations
- *Exploration*—deliberately widening our horizons.

How does one use this information? Plutchik says that there is a particular sequence of events that leads to an emotion:

1. *Stimulus Event* (what stirs us up)
2. *Cognition* (what it means to us)
3. *Feeling* (what our body tells us)
4. *Behavior* (what do we do about it)
5. *Function* (how it affects our survival).

Here are some examples he offers as a model to help analyze important situations:

- *Stimulus* (threat by enemy); *cognition* (danger); *feeling* (fear); *behavior* (run); *function* (protection).
- *Stimulus* (loss of parent); *cognition* (isolation); *feeling* (sadness); *behavior* (cry for help); *function* (reintegration).

Are there any important events you want to analyze? Plutchik suggests that the primary and mixed emotions are these:

- *Optimism:* anticipation and joy; *love:* joy and acceptance; *submission:* acceptance and fear; *awe:* fear and surprise; *disappointment:* surprise and sadness; *remorse:* disgust and sadness; *contempt:* anger and disgust; *aggressiveness:* anger and anticipation, and so back to the beginning.

FEELING GOOD AND BAD

Why should any feelings develop at all, except to signal us to run like hell because the nearest saber-toothed tiger is making noises as though he is hungry? There are two ideas which are useful in understanding the pleasant–unpleasant dimension of our emotional life:

1. There is a built-in reward and punishment system.
2. Feelings represent signals to us as to what to remember and why.

Reward system. Studies of brain anatomy and chemistry

reveal that our emotional life is dependent upon the nature of the functioning of particular chemicals (neurohormones and neurotransmitters) which bring information from one part of the nervous system to the next. Here we are particularly interested in the nervous system of the limbic lobe and the pleasure centers. I don't want to enter into the controversy as to how much we control it or if it controls us. However, understanding the mechanism of human feelings will help you to determine whether something is defective in your reactions. It may offer leads as to how to correct it.

The feelings of *excitement* can be brought about either by natural events or artificially through particular brain chemicals called catecholamines. Many events usually stimulate their production, but when things are dull some of us turn to coffee, cocaine, or amphetamines ("speed"). In fact, according to the science section of the *New York Times* (1/22/80), even love can create a "high" through causing our brain to secrete a substance related to "speed" (phenylethelamine). It is the demand for this "high" (apparently with the frustration of unsuitable relationships) which motivates some people into intense love situations.

When we associate the pleasures of excitement with situations that are ultimately self-destructive, the temporary pleasure of being "high" (caused by your defective brain) encourages you into damaging activities. If you feel good diving out of an airplane or racing your car, you stimulate catecholamines which maintain this behavior, at the potential cost of disaster.

Becoming *satisfied* is different from excitement or pleasant anticipation. Probably you have read about how the brain creates its own opiates (morphinelike peptides called enkephalins, endorphins, etc.). What these substances seem to do is calm us down when we are upset, or offer us the feeling that a state of needing something has been gratified. The normal brain manufactures these reinforcers of good feelings. For most of us, even when conditions are bad, small rewards can relieve our spirits (music, nature, a friendly word). In fact, these opiatelike substances seem to be one of the chemicals described in Chapter 3 whose long-lasting effects tie together a variety of events long after a situation would seem to have occurred and been finished (Gurin, 1979). It is thought that the formation of human bonds, e.g., between child and parent, lovers, friends, evolves from the feeling of gratification associated with the release of an endorphin. After a while the presence of a particular person is anticipated with pleasure.

Feelings and information. What good are feelings? To let us know what is happening to us! By pointing out pleasure and pain, feelings help us to select and remember those parts of our environment, particular people, situations, and events which affect our welfare. This helps us to remember, since we can pay attention to and remember only a limited amount of information. What took place before and during good or bad feelings *reinforces* or *deconditions* our tendencies to repeat or avoid certain actions. As information comes in, our reaction to it is toned by these peptides, which make the brain more or less responsive to information coming in in conventional ways (vision, hearing, bodily states). We pick out and remember stimuli occurring in the presence of these chemicals which ordinarily might be ignored or forgotten.

When the system needs repair. Some of us have reward systems that do not provide pleasure. The serious mental illness known as schizophrenia is characterized by *anhedonia*, i.e., many afflicted people enjoy no pleasure. In some kinds of depression, people cannot enjoy themselves or relieve their mood. This is illustrated by the following vignette from a brain chemistry researcher at Wyeth Laboratories, Larry Stein: "That abnormal brain of a depressive must be quite abnormal, indeed. When a successful businessman who has a nice family and everything going for him walks out the window one day—that's bad chemistry."

Another instance of the reward system functioning defectively occurs when the individual rewards himself/herself in ways which violate particular goals. Somebody may be very lonely but dissipate the feelings of discomfort through masturbation or solitary eating. Consequently, other people are not associated with the feeling of relief (Westermeyer, Bush, and Wintrob, 1978). Little motivation develops to form new social contacts or approach particular people who might be available.

CONSTITUTION AND TEMPERAMENT

There are long-lasting qualities in your personality, which are appreciably determined by heredity (although not exclusively), which shape the nature of your reactions, how much energy you possess, your stamina, your disposition, and many other qualities that can be called nonverbal, lacking mental content, and not involved with motivation, goals, or identity.

Constitution. This is defined by R. M. Goldenson in *The Encyclopedia of Human Behavior* as "the relatively enduring biological make-up of an individual, in part due to heredity, and in part to life experience and environmental factors." The supporting functions of strength and energy, health and reactivity, which are important contributors to adaptation, are included in constitution. The lucky person with a strong constitution has endurance, health, and resistance to disease and stress. He faces difficulties without collapsing or developing psychosomatic illnesses or emotional discomforts. The person with a weaker constitution is vulnerable to illness, is unable to perform under stress without fatigue, ulcers, heart attacks, and emotional discomfort. It is important that you evaluate your constitution, improve your health where possible, and then set definite limits beyond which you will not force yourself to go except in emergencies.

Most popularizers of psychological self-help, as well as theorists of psychotherapy, have stressed the mental aspect of adaptation and change. This approach is one-sided and partially incorrect. You will be severely hampered if you guide yourself according to such pap and ignore the body which carries your beloved psyche. Mental functioning is enhanced by either a strong body or activity which respects your limitations and tries to overcome them. Think of Beethoven or Helen Keller (deaf), Steinmetz (crippled), or Franklin Roosevelt (paralyzed). These magnificent human beings developed courage and stamina to compensate for the frailties of their bodies. What do I do? I try to jog three times a week for an hour. Without this *investment* in my body, I would not withstand the many pressures on me or I would be less productive.

Temperament. Goldenson defines temperament as "a general term for emotional make-up including characteristic energy level, moods and mood changes, intensity and tempo of reactions to people and situations." Betz and Thomas (1979) add that it involves feeling-tone rather than the way we see the world. It reflects bodily functions which serve the aims of preserving our species and maintaining our well-being. Our temperament is carried out by ancient neurophysiological systems. These create significant differences between people in their bodily reactivity (Bakal, 1975, citing Lacey and Lacy, 1958). There are familiar emotional qualities that are the results of differences in temperament, e.g., when we describe people as phlegmatic, indifferent (cold-blooded), calm (even-tempered), irascible (hot-blooded), choleric, sensitive, volatile, energetic, reflective, or practical (Betz and Thomas, 1979).

Thomas and Chess (1977) have shown that infants differ from each other—right from the beginning of life. They say that temperament has to do with *style*, i.e., *how* we do things, not *why* (our motives) or *what* (our abilities or the content of our mind). They think that it is affected by heredity (p. 136). This is supported by the anthropological studies of Daniel G. Freedman (1979), who showed that the reactions of children of different ethnic backgrounds to different stresses were similar within their groups, but varied between groups. In some ways, newborn Navajos, North and South Chinese, Caucasians, and Japanese-American babies all did their own thing when confined, or had a cloth put over their nose, or were dropped a few inches. Our distinctive qualities at birth:

- Determine whether we find our environment suitable for our early personality and reactions
- Help shape our parents' reactions to us (Anneliese Korner, 1973)
- Influence whether we become more or less welcome visitors to our household depending upon whether we are as children "easy" (to handle), "difficult," or "slow to warm up" (Chess and Thomas, 1973; Thomas and Chess, 1977; Thomas, Chess, and Birch, 1969).

What are the personality traits (temperament) with which we come into the world? How do they relate to adult life?

1. *Activity level.* People differ in their amount of activity, the pace at which they function, and how they perform muscular acts. As children, we vary in our response to being bathed and fed, while as adults we differ from being very inactive to tearing around all over the map.

2. *Rhythmicity.* This means how regular or predictable are we? Some of us are so stable that we can be used to set watches

by, while others vary in our activities from moment to moment.

3. *Approach or withdrawal.* This describes the child's or adult's initial attitude toward new situations, such as people, food, or procedures. Some of us are reluctant to confront anything new, while others are eager for a change of scene and faces.

4. *Adaptability.* We can't always choose our environment, particularly not our business associates, family, and teachers. Thus we must be alert to any inability in coping with change or new situations.

5. *Threshold of responsiveness.* How much of a poke is necessary to cause us to spring (or drag) into action? Consider the difference between the person who jumps up with fists raised when someone looks cross-eyed at him, and the indolent guy who can be stepped on without objecting.

6. *Intensity of reaction.* People differ in the amount of energy they put into a reaction. This differs from paragraph 1 (activity level) in that it refers to what happens in a given act, not the overall extent of activity. Think of the phlegmatic wilted-lettuce-leaf handshake versus the Bull of the Pampas who sends you to your local chiropractor!

7. *Quality of mood.* We have seen how significant this is, i.e., it is the aspect of our life which often concerns us most: how much pleasant, joyful, friendly feeling there is, as contrasted with unpleasant, depressed and unfriendly reactions.

8. *Distractibility.* How effective are outside events in interfering with what you are doing? When I write, I put aside practically everything except my responsibilities to my clients. On the other hand, noises which are nuisances, created by people for their own convenience at my expense, could make me angry and distract me.

9. *Attention span and persistence.* Are you persistent, or maladaptive? Goal-oriented or self-destructive? Obviously, persistence can be enjoyed or hated, according to whether you are the beneficiary or the victim of it, the successful plodder or the outraged mother.

Reactions to New Situations

What is your style? Whatever it is, it may have started when you were in kindergarten. Has it changed? Thomas and Chess

(1977, pp. 95–96) think kids fall into these types. What about yourself?

1. The *plunger* plunges into new activities quickly, positively, and unhesitantly (dives into a pool without being dead certain it's filled).

2. The *go-alonger* goes along in a positive manner, but does not plunge right in (waits until the car he buys has been in production at least ten years).

3. The *non-participator* stays a non-participant in a new situation for weeks or months (self-appointed wallflower).

4. The *sideliner* stands on the sidelines waiting, then slowly and gradually gets involved in the new activity (waits for the gold-engraved invitation).

Some teachers overestimate the intelligence of "plungers" and underestimate the intelligence of "sideliners," and since teacher's approval is the equivalent of the Nobel Prize in physics, your style does make a difference!

Significance of constitutional and temperamental traits.
These traits form the supporting skeleton for all other activities in life. Children (and of course adults) may develop generally under conditions which are dissonant (lack of harmony) with their temperaments. On the other hand, they may experience demands consistent with their capacities, which teaches them self-mastery.

EMOTIONAL METABOLISM

It is possible to think of your emotional life as having similarities to the physiology of your body. In the *anabolic state*, the body is building up, and we have a sense of well-being and strength. In the *catabolic state*, we feel sick and weak, and believe that the body has betrayed us. *Physiological metabolism* is a balance between growth and tearing down. We can conceive of *emotional metabolism* as the balance of healthy and self-destructive functioning in the personality area. People frequently disregard this balance between constructive and destructive existence. Do you disregard the elements of self-protection, survival, or good mental health?

The questionnaire on page 52 has proven useful in offering insight into the balance between constructive (anabolic) and destructive (catabolic) forces in people's lifestyles. This self-assessment will alert you to:

- Areas of strength which you can use and develop as resources and morale-builders at times of stress
- Aspects of your personality which are worth developing in order to have a more fulfilled and constructive lifestyle
- Signs of stress which reveal the presence of destructive people and/or situations in your life.

INSTRUCTIONS FOR EMOTIONAL METABOLISM QUESTIONNAIRE

Follow these instructions for the questionnaire that appears on page 52.

1. In the area of *Personal Development* place a check underneath the number which corresponds to your evaluation of your development or need for growth in each area. Then add up the total number of points, which gives you a Personal Development Score. Place this number at "A" below.

2. Place a check next to each of the *Signs of Stress* you have. Add up the checks, and place the quantity at "B" below.

3. Place a check next to each of the *Creative/Productive Blocks* that you show. Add up the checks and place the quantity at "C" below.

4. Subtract emotional catabolic points ("B" and "C" from *Personal Development* "A"). This will give you an idea whether your emotional life is constructive or self-destructive, depending upon whether the sum is positive or negative.

EMOTIONAL METABOLISM QUESTIONNAIRE

PERSONAL DEVELOPMENT

Place a check underneath the number which corresponds to your evaluation of your development or need for growth in these areas of personal fulfillment.

(4) Completely fulfilled   (3) Very well developed   (2) Needs a lot of work
(1) Little satisfaction   (0) My development is inadequate

	(4)	(3)	(2)	(1)	(0)
Capacity for deep experience					
Striving for meaningful goals					
I accept others on their terms					
I accept my own worth					
I form satisfactory relationships					
Autonomy/enjoyment of my activities					
I have developed my potential					
I have self-awareness/clear identity					

(TOTAL) ____ (A) (Place at "A" below)

SIGNS OF STRESS

____ Bodily symptoms
        (psychosomatic)
____ Anxiety or fear
____ Guilt/feelings of unworthiness
____ Tension and irritability
____ Frequent or constant anger or
        rage
____ Fatigue
____ Sexual problems
____ Dissatisfied/emotionally
        deprived
____ Rejection/humiliation/
        vulnerability
____ Job dissatisfaction
____ Sleep problems/bad dreams
____ Apathy/indifference
____ Unpleasant fantasies
____ Overload/inability to cope
____ Helplessness/hopelessness/
        depression
____ Recent loss of mate/family
        member/status

____ TOTAL (Place at "B" below)

CREATIVE/PRODUCTIVE BLOCKS

____ Fear of taking risks
____ Unclear identity/sense of self/
        goals
____ Requires direction from others
____ Excessively high standards
____ Lack of competence
____ Weak motivation
____ Poor work habits
____ Sabotage success
____ Fear of changing lifestyle
____ Low self-esteem reduces
        performance
____ Rebellious against legitimate
        authority
____ Bad models tilt you toward
        failure
____ Fear of success
____ Lack of self-assertiveness
____ Poor use of time
____ Unfinished business prevents
        achievement of goals

____ TOTAL (Place at "C" below)

Add up the number of points:
(A) Personal Development Score ____ (−); (B) Signs of Stress ____ (−);
(C) Blocks ____
+ = Emotionally Anabolic: Work on Personal Development
− = Emotionally Catabolic: Work on Reducing Self-Destructiveness

6) Stress: Emotional Battle Fatigue

Let us review some common kinds of stress so that you will be able to avoid situations that will wear you out and potentially lead to disaster. Your goal will be to:

- Identify signs of stress in your life
- Recognize cause and effect
- Understand your particular vulnerability
- Avoid these situations where possible
- Cope with them better where necessary.

DEFINITION OF STRESS

Stress can be defined as a very difficult situation, momentary or long-lasting, with which it is difficult for yout to cope. It can also be a change in your world for which your usual modes of adaptation don't succeed. There are various ways that stress shows itself: physiological, medical, and psychological.

CAUSES OF STRESS

Stress has many sources, for example:

- Frustration of basic needs
- Damage to self-esteem
- Fright or threat of physical injury
- Requirement to perform beyond one's capacity for a long period.

Early signs of stress can be feelings of emotional distress. Later results of stress can be psychosis, serious psychosomatic illness that ultimately becomes permanent or life-threatening, or persistent anxiety, depression, or sleep disorders. The source of stress can be a direct reaction to events, anticipation of forthcoming trouble, or a persistent symptom long after a traumatic experience.

RECOGNIZING STRESS

The first step is to be able to recognize danger. According to Chinese sages, of the thirty-six ways of averting disaster, running away is the best! It is also true that people who prepare themselves for disaster frequently survive it, e.g., by attending to instructions on boarding an airplane (*Human Behavior,* January 1979, p. 24).

By recognizing the particular stresses in your life, you will be able to make constructive changes. Perhaps seeing in print the statement that particular events are genuinely destructive will enable you to give up any false sense of courage. You may also receive solace from the fact that the painful events of your life have occurred to numerous other people, and the difficulties and discomforts that you have experienced are universal events. You will also have a deeper understanding and compassion for the people around you.

WHY STRESS?

Particular personality constellations seem to experience certain kinds of illness. It seems likely that the way they create or handle certain emotions contributes to their vulnerability. Individuals also have different degrees of bodily reactivity of different organs: blood vessels and heart, the digestive, sexual, and muscular systems. These cause larger or smaller responses than average, resulting in different degrees of self-awareness in different situations. In addition, varying capacities for physiological reaction would make these organs more or less likely to be vulnerable to disease or susceptible to conditioning.

SOME PSYCHOLOGICAL FACTORS WHICH AFFECT THE DEGREE OF STRESS

The meaning we give to situations. Our reaction makes the difference between whether or not an experience has the effect of stress. I happen to enjoy traveling by ocean liner. It gives me pleasure to feel the rocking of the ship. It makes me at one with the sea. Result: excitement. To others, movement disturbs their sense of stability. It is possible that they have a more sensitive inner ear. Result. *Mal de mer.*

Hans Selye (1976), the great pioneer of the concept of stress, defines it as any demand made upon the body (or mind). Continued demands upon our body or mind for performance or survival eventually lead to pathological or reduced functioning. Selye discriminates between *distress* (harmful) and *eustress* (beneficial), reminding us that the effects of many events depend upon "how we take them."

Disturbance of homeostasis. The body generally keeps our physiological reactions within quite narrow limits. For example, oxygen level is maintained by pulse rate, arterial constriction, rate of breathing, and availability of red blood cells. When we anticipate or experience trouble, the demand for oxygen goes up and a variety of physiological responses occur to ensure that our oxygen level is adequate. After a short period, the various organs return to a relatively stable, normal level of response. However, any persistent requirement for performance, an unpleasant emotional environment (real or symbolic danger), or difficult external environment (e.g., cold, heat, requirement for excessive effort) can eventually lead to stress and organ damage. Some bodily reactions occur (e.g., in our cardiovascular system) even though we do not realize that we are responding to some outside event such as a telephone ringing (Bakal, 1975).

Inhibited actions. In the good old days, when all we had to face were poisonous snakes, saber-tooth tigers, glaciers, and other natural events, we knew whether our best interests were *fight* or *flight*. Today, we may be in *conflict* as to what to do, since we may feel the consequence of both courses of action to be too costly. Consequently, in addition to William James's famous alternatives, we have to add the possibility of *brake* (with the motor running and our body in gear). This state of being "aroused," or "vigilant," but unable to take off in all directions is especially troublesome. As I was writing this a woman called me up, voice trembling, because she didn't know whether to pursue her plan of calling an attorney to get a separation from her husband. She had a great deal of resentment toward him, but he was trying to turn over a new leaf and making a great point of the improvement in their relationship. She didn't know what to do. I advised her that while time would resolve the conflict in one way or another, she could actually take a step in either direction and see how she felt. I suggested that waiting too long for a solution was likely to be harmful to her.

Whether we express our feelings. An emotional release is stress-reducing. Women are less likely to suffer stress-related illnesses than men on similar jobs, because women find it easier to vent their emotions and verbalize their frustrations, according to psychiatrist Irving H. Bracer (*Human Behavior*, January 1979, p. 34).

Emotional support. This can also sensitize workers to such special dangers as fumes and dust. Whether or not workers' health will suffer can depend upon whether they received emotional support at home or from their supervisor. For example, workers who received support were less likely to break out in a rash from exposure to chemicals (Gunnar G. Sevelius quoted in the *New York Times*, Shabccoff).

Whether we experience control. The effects of stress and becoming depressed have a lot in common, including the belief that a situation is beyond control (we believe that our best efforts will not influence the outcome in a beneficial way or avert pain or some kind of damage). When people learn that they can control some events or people, they then learn how to escape from the situation or avoid its harmful effects. If they believe that they have no control ("*learned helplessness*"), then they may not bother to adapt successfully or to learn useful ways of preventing damage to themselves. Even in dealing with bureaucrats this principle holds: When we believe that the *impersonal system or regulations* are at fault, then we may accede to a disagreeable decision. On the other hand, when one believes that one is dealing with an *individual* who has perpetrated something disagreeable, then we might try to influence them, or conversely, feel even worse about being refused (Glass and Singer, 1972).

Self-deception. Unwillingness to admit that we are anxious can lead to the result that the objective signs of anxiety are even greater (heart rate, sweat gland activity, and forehead muscle tension). Ordinarily we can control our anxiety directly, or reduce the pressure upon us. When we deny the presence of

distress, then we "deregulate" our control over our bodily functions (Schwartz, 1980) and our bodily reactions can become substantially more disturbed. This in turn leads to fatigue and
ultimately to psychosomatic disorders.

SOURCES OF STRESS

Humanity is poorly adapted to the civilized world. The evidence comes from the high rates of crime and mental illness.
Rapid change and the breakdown of the family are both symptoms and causes. Let us analyze the sources of stress in a careful way. By studying them, you can determine which affect you.
You will discover those situations in which you are most vulnerable and then be able to take effective corrective action.

   1. Directly work related. These are situations in which the
working conditions and people are clearly putting pressure on
our self-esteem and strength. In some cases the work itself
would be stressful to anyone. In others, we are in the wrong job
for a person of our capabilities, temperament, personality, and
interest. In the first section, I will discuss various ways in which
a job can be overwhelming. In the second, I will point out how
we can recognize a mismatch between ourselves and a particular position.

   • *Performance overload.* Anyone would collapse when there
is an insufficient work force to accomplish the assignment within the assigned time. I know a report writer for a famous business credit rating company who was required to write fifty-one
reports per week, including time spent on the telephone and
going to company offices for information. He fell behind, and
spent time at home writing, despite difficulties with his wife.
When the quota was increased, he demanded either another
assignment or that he be fired. He got a better job in which he
is doing very well!

   • *Sensory overload.* Too much information of different kinds
is coming in at once. When we have to sort out all these stimuli,
separate those which are important from those that are irrelevant, and then make decisions, stress is created. There is an
optimal level of stimulation for us with boredom occurring
when not enough change takes place, and over-arousal when
there is too much damage for us to handle.

• *Role overload.* Sometimes we have to deal with too many different kinds of people, perform a great variety of tasks, go into different departments, or meet with people in different professions. When this happens, very rapid changes are required, and a great variety of professional and social skills are called upon. We do not always have this capability.

• *Culture shock.* Alvin Toffler (1970) pointed out that the rate of technological change is becoming more rapid with every generation. Our job skills can be out-of-date before we leave school, or shortly after we start a job. To obtain retraining, we might have to give up opportunities for rest and relaxation, adding to fatigue.

• *Ambiguity and uncertainty.* When we don't know exactly what we ought to in order to do our jobs well, we may feel that our employer doesn't support us. People get anxious in such a condition, and frequently are tempted to leave their jobs because of this type of stress.

• *Role conflict.* In contrast to uncertainty as to what is expected, this means that we are required to do different things that are incompatible with each other. We feel torn by conflicts between different people, or must get along with people whom we dislike.

• *Powerlessness.* Inability to participate in our employer's decision-making processes means that we are left out of plans that affect us. People with this reaction often are absent from their jobs, feel very dissatisfied, work inefficiently, and eventually quit.

• *Pressure to conform.* This is a kind of thought control in which ideas, style, and attitudes have to conform to the norms of the place where we work. We feel that our identity is violated. This attitude is self-destructive to our employer, since when people feel that only certain ideas are valuable, then they stop making any contribution. They feel afraid, keep their feelings to themselves, have difficulty in saying what they mean, and tend to give in rather than offer new ideas.

• *Damage to self-esteem.* Some superiors use degradation as a management device, or else express their neurosis through downgrading their subordinates. If you are unable to express your anger at this treatment appropriately, or cannot be self-assertive and thus control your supervisor, then stress becomes very strong.

• *Mismatch between the person and the job.* This is the case when you are technically competent, but your style of handling people, information, and tasks is not suitable for your present position. I have heard it asserted by many personnel directors that about nine out of ten people who get fired are terminated for a mismatch, not because of incompetence.

• *Incompatibility of temperament with the position.* Stress occurs when our work niche makes excessive social, physical, emotional, and stamina demands upon us. For example, a shy person who must meet new people, or a muscular and active person in a white-collar desk job.

• *Information handling.* People prefer particular kinds of problems to solve. Moreover, when each of us is given a task, we go about it in unique ways. For example, one person works out the nature of a problem, but doesn't want to work out the details. Somebody else would be glad to be told what the problem is, and could then discover how to solve it. When we are working, we have a definite preference for a degree of structure, i.e., how specific the instructions should be for us to perform our duties. There are also differences between people in their preference for the amount of stimulation that goes on at once; some of us like change and turmoil, while others prefer quiet and predictability.

• *Contact with others.* This can be stressful in a variety of ways: (1) we have to do our work with people whose styles and responsibilities we really don't understand; (2) we are responsible for getting other people to do their job; (3) we don't get along well with others. If we are not good at working with people, then the requirement that we influence others to get their jobs done or to help us perform our own duties can make us want to get a job as a beachcomber!

• *Incompetence.* Yes, once in a while even the best of us just aren't smart enough or knowledgeable enough to do our job well. We may have been promoted to a position whose requirements we haven't mastered. Perhaps the real nature of the job has been misrepresented. The standards of the position we have been holding could have been raised. It might be that technological change makes our skills less valuable. Certainly, to be incompetent for our job is an appropriate source of anxiety.

2. Reduced competence. These are conditions that reduce our ability to handle life's events. Consequently, some events that would usually be ignored or coped with easily become stressful or impossible to deal with.

• *Illness.* Disease, weakness, fatigue, high temperature, or the side effects of medications can hamper our ability to deal with problems.

• *Brain damage.* Head injuries, inflammation of the brain, high fever, toxic chemicals, cerebral atrophy can reduce overall competence or ability to handle relatively specific areas. The use of alcohol can produce irreversible brain damage. (It is controversial as to which level of usage produces this effect.)

• *Psychedelic and psychotropic drugs.* Marijuana, cocaine, hashish, heroin, minor tranquilizers, etc., can have unfortunate effects upon sleep, efficiency, alertness, and motivation.

• *Fatigue.* This is the most important stressor because it leads to inefficiency and susceptibility to disease. *Fatigue increases our vulnerability to any other kind of stress.*

• *Trauma.* This is defined as a sudden, unexpected, overwhelming experience. The result of trauma can last for a long period, even when there has been only a threat and no apparent damage, or long after the danger is past. Victims of trauma often show depression, anxiety, bodily reactions, nightmares, disturbing fantasies, increased sensitivity to threat, and feelings of humiliation.

3. Community, family, and lifestyle. These are the stresses of daily living. Some companies are located in college-campus style grounds, while others are in a heavy industrial environment with unpleasant urban routes. The same is true for our personal community. Some of the common stresses of daily living include:

• *Environmental stress.* Difficulties with travel, crowding, crime, noise, ethnic and social heterogeneity. The business cycle has been associated with rates of suicide, admissions to mental hospitals, cardiovascular illnesses, imprisonment, homicide, cirrhosis of the liver.

• *Rapid change.* Even familiar events in daily life can be disturbing. For example, vacations, marriages, and changes of residence make us vulnerable to physical illness. The greater the change and the disturbance it causes, and the less that you can adapt, the greater the likelihood of developing disease. Some new responses to stress, e.g., alcohol or drugs, or sexual problems where none existed, create additional stresses.

• *Threat*. There are life-situations in which physical or emotional abuse is frequent or threatened. Some communities are populated by many dangerous characters. People are verbally or physically abused as they go back and forth to work. Threat also occurs in some households. One member may be a bully, or the entire emotional atmosphere can be described as abusive (see Parker, 1972a).

• *Boredom*. To some extent boredom is usually the responsibility of the bored person. While some jobs, mates, friends, parents, or children are emotionally depleting and offer little intellectual or emotional nourishment, some people have never learned to generate their own ideas and/or to feed themselves intellectually and emotionally. They are overly dependent upon others (Parker, 1978).

• *Frustration*. This differs from boredom insofar as a person perceives what he/she wants, but is prevented from obtaining it. One may think of the sexually frustrating marriage, the employer who does not reward good efforts, and the executive who cannot express his abilities because of the lack of appropriate facilities in his organization.

• *Degradation*. People frequently stay in situations with arrogant supervisors, critical mates and children, and friends, who in the guise of a relationship are needlessly critical. Many people are trained to believe that it is useless or damaging to express their anger (Parker, 1972b) and therefore cannot fight back or express their feelings in a way that reduces the other party's abusiveness. Thus the stressful situation remains, or becomes worse when the bully is upset by not having a fight!

• *Separation*. The loss of a person or group upon whom we depend for love is a common cause of depression and loneliness. Since this situation is uncontrollable, the loss has added to it a blow to our self-esteem due to our powerlessness. Separation can create feelings of weakness since we have learned from birth to depend upon others. For some, to lose a mate, friend, or job causes a loss of identity. One person I knew, when her sister was moving to another part of the country, burst into tears when she saw a questionnaire item which asked "Who are you?" "What kind of a question is that?" she asked. "Right now I am nobody!"

4. Internally generated stress. These are the circumstances in which we are our own worst enemy. There can be an internal battle between forces representing different elements of our upbringing, weaknesses caused by unhappy moods, etc.

• *Internal conflicts.* We give ourselves opposite signals at the same time. "Do this—because it's good; stop—you will be punished." Or, "One parent told me I was good so I can relate to people; wait—my other parent told me I'm bad, so I'm going to be rejected." Or, "If I do what my conscience tells me is right for this job, my supervisor will get upset."

• *Disturbed mood.* Any of the unhappy feelings related to signs of stress can discourage us or interfere with our efficiency. Anxiety, anger, depression, tension, and all of the rest are both signs of, and causes for, further stress. There can be an exception: When these feelings motivate us to change our personality or situation or to make any change, including the best one—get out!

• *Self-degradation.* People frequently feed themselves hostile thoughts: "I am no good, rotten, evil, incompetent, unlikable, inadequate." Identifying oneself in this way creates depression, low self-esteem, and other unhappy/disturbed moods. They create further stress because they lead to a masochistic attitude: (1) staying in situations that are degrading or stressful, and (2) disbelieving positive statements to them or successes that would reinforce a constructive attitude or lifestyle. Furthermore, self-degrading individuals do not create situations in which success is likely.

• *Discouragement.* Consistent failure, a masochistic attitude, or a real, or imagined, sense of powerlessness leads to the belief that one cannot succeed, that any effort is too much work. Individuals in this frame of mind let situations get worse. Should they review their lifestyle or plight they find that they are in worse shape than before. The cycle of anxiety-failure-added stress continues.

• *Disturbed thinking.* At the beginning of serious illness, or due to the use of drugs (sometimes the effects are long-lasting, or return unexpectedly), people may see their world as strange, changed, frightening, or disintegrating. They experience themselves and their surroundings as unfamiliar and threatening. This reaction creates further disorganization.

• *Excessively high standards.* Sometimes we place very great demands on ourselves because of our reaction to early experiences. Our parents may have had great expectations of us. We may have felt degraded and have created the illusion that by being exceptionally effective we will convince those old-time figures in our life that we are really OK. Perhaps we believe that achievement is the way to get love. As a result, we may never complete a job because we don't believe that it is ever ready to pass into the hands of the next person in the process. If you think that you can be a better fiddler than Heifetz, relax. Develop your talents, not your competitiveness.

7) Toward Social Understanding

By now you are aware that sophisticated understanding of your own finely honed, complexly functioning mind is not enough to keep you out of trouble. The people around you do have some slight effect upon your emotional well-being, so let's explore some of the ways of increasing your sensitivity to what is happening around you. You will find it useful to apply your knowledge of stress to various common social events.

I want you to be more aware of the nuances of social events. Then you will be able to avert stress before it becomes excessive. You will also recognize constructive experiences and the people who should be encouraged to be with you. Oh, yes, while it is delightful that you are becoming aware of your own needs, do try to be aware of what the other person wants out of life as well.

I asked one of my discussion groups to speak about avoidable self-destructive behavior, and a great number of comments involved social relationships. Here are some examples:

- "I'm going to stop running a blood bank for vampires."
- "My self-confidence takes a beating from time to time. I want to be more reliable to myself so that I can depend on myself if my rights are abused."
- A mental health professional said that "I get along well with patients but I fight with the staff."
- "I shouldn't have entered my marriage. I made a serious error. I separated after thirty-five years. It was the best decision ever. I just needed somebody then, and she came along. I told myself not to do it."

• "My friend is trying to conform me to his ideas. I was dependent on him. Now I'm trying to rely on myself and not do what he wants."

• "I tried to make myself like this person who liked me a lot. I had to cut it off, as it would have made me feel even worse."

• "I tell women off, and women don't call me again."

• "I can avoid self-destructive experiments if I just deal with the people whose company I value and have nothing to do with the rest."

• "I'm in a stressful situation at work. The staff under me is hostile and there is no communication. I feel like going through the door, but I need a job."

• "I realize that some of my friends are not good for me. I have to start over and get them out of my life."

• "I stayed with a man who would only spend one day a week with me. When he died it was painful but a release."

• "I have been seeing a woman for a year. She is insensitive and hurting. I told her I'm going to find somebody who appreciates me."

EMOTIONAL NEEDS

I define emotional needs as experiences we crave which are better satisfied by other people than by ourselves. Therefore, although emotional needs are very personal, their effect upon our social life makes them a very important part of a chapter on social understanding. It is a tremendous error to believe that everybody has the same needs, and therefore no further thinking is necessary. In a general sense this is true, and the list I propose of basic emotional needs would be agreed upon by most people, but that is only the beginning! Each of us has had different experiences of fulfillment, frustration, and expectations in these areas. We bring these into new relationships. They shape the outcome, because of the experiences we had long before we met our partners. Thus, it is vital that we begin to understand in what way we are satisfied or frustrated in various areas, and who we really think ought to fulfill us. (I will tell you in advance that if you rely upon a partner to make you feel good you are in trouble, big trouble.)

Good relationships evolve from your understanding of, and

willingness to meet the deeply felt needs of the people you associate with. Conversely, should you realize that you cannot meet the needs of someone in a significant way, you might feel that it is more prudent not to set up expectations that will be frustrated.

THE EMOTIONAL QUESTIONNAIRE

1. Your emotional state. For each of these needs rate your degree of satisfaction as *frustrated, moderately dissatisfied,* or *content.*

2. Who is to meet your needs? There are several possibilities for coping with frustrated needs. You can decide that you should largely meet your own needs in a particular area. This would be a degree of autonomy. You might decide that a sexual partner ought to be the one to meet this need. Finally, you may feel that some other person or several other people might be the source of fulfillment, e.g., friends, some other sexual partner, family, or co-workers. Indicate the degree to which you expect each source of fulfillment to be important for each need: *Almost Completely, Moderately, Not Very Much* (AC; M; NVM).

Need	*Satisfaction*	*Dissatisfaction to be met by*		
		Self	*Partner*	*Others*
Companionship	————	———	———	———
Recognition/Esteem	————	———	———	———
Love	————	———	———	———
Security	————	———	———	———
Intimacy/Closeness	————	———	———	———
Sex	————	———	———	———

Try to be aware whether there is a balance in your expectations of satisfaction between yourself, an intimate partner, and the world in general. To crave too much from one person is to make demands which can irritate the last person you intend to antagonize, and self-destructively cause someone to leave you alone. Conversely, if you are a very self-sufficient person, though presumably with some social needs, you will be experienced as frustrating by someone whose sense of personal value is increased by the opportunity to be loving and useful to another person. A suitable partner for you might be an equally self-sufficient individual.

KINDS OF COMMUNICATION

Individuals express their feelings and experience life on many levels. One convenient way of regarding the different aspects of experience and communication is dividing it into verbal, nonverbal, and unconscious.

Verbal. The use of words to express feelings and ideas is certainly the kind of expression that people take most seriously, both in using them and in understanding others. Words are probably the best way to explain certain ideas. They are indispensable in writing laws, contracts, and menus. Nevertheless, the person who relies completely on words to present his feelings and attitudes comes across as dry, uninteresting, and occasionally insincere or lacking insight.

Nevertheless, even though I will describe other means of "reading" people, I place great emphasis on words. They have a potential clarity not shared by other means of expression. When I deal with people, professionally or personally, I am a great questioner. If I am not sure, I ask. However, once I have ascertained what I consider to be a clear-cut meaning or commitment, I assume that this is what the other party intends. Therefore, I recommend that the reader not try to be a mind reader. Rather, if some message is unclear or devious, ask the person to clarify or to repeat. Do not be ashamed to state that you do not understand. Some individuals deliberately develop a devious or confusing style in order to mislead you. Others have been conditioned to avoid expressing their feelings or attitudes clearly, because they have been punished as children for being themselves. Yet, you should encourage others to speak to you clearly and sincerely. If they do not, then you must make yourself aware that this is the case.

Nonverbal. A great deal of meaning is communicated without the use of words. For example, research has indicated that our expectations of the success or failure of children in school or at swimming lessons have a marked effect upon their actual performance. The tone of voice in which instructions are given also can change ratings. Research indicates that movements of the face, body, head, hands, and legs are significantly associated with emotional reactions, or give information useful for the alert observer (Dittman, undated manuscript; Hall, Rosenthal, Archer, DiMatteo and Rogers, 1978). It is asserted that females are more sensitive readers of nonverbal cues, but everyone knows that women are more intuitive! What groups are generally the least responsive to these subtle sources of information? Trailing the lists are clinicians such as myself (psychiatrists, clinical psychologists, physicians, psychiatric nurses, and other mental health workers), followed by teachers, and last, business executives. Pillars of the community. Curiously, romantic couples whose skills were most dissimilar are most likely to be together. Why? They know they don't understand each other, so they had better make clear what is going on. Either that, or opposites attract. Take your choice.

How do others make a nonverbal impression on us? One thinks immediately of body build, vigor, strength, and weight. Considerable information is conveyed by a statement that a man is very tall, undernourished, slender, but seemingly very active and strong. A woman might be described as of average height, overweight, broadly built, inactive, or flabby. There might be seeming contradictions which tell a story—the obese person who remains strong and active, the slender person who has let his muscles deteriorate.

Physical appearance also tells a story. We observe complexion, aesthetic impression, and whether there are any disabilities. Racial identification, clear or pockmarked skin, and degrees of sunburn or pallor are information provided by the complexion. The conformity between cultural stereotypes of beauty and the actual "looks" of a man or woman will affect how they are received socially and could influence you in ways which are not in your best interest. Also, there is a harsh, threatening quality, easily detected, in the person who is looking for the opportunity to be brutal.

There is a great deal to be learned from a person's *handshake*. I recently shook hands with a man whom I met on the street. He had been part of a group that treated me insincerely and deviously. As I reached toward his hand, he partially withdrew his as though there were slime on mine. All this was supposed to be concealed by his usual big, congealed smile. Did he take me in? No. The directness of the handshake, its artificial forcefulness or weakness will reveal much about the underlying intentions of the person in the relationship. It will also be useful to find out if the person is anxious, e.g., whether his hands are cold or sweaty. Since circulatory disorders might contribute to these conditions, if in doubt, ask! You might reveal yourself as a concerned person by determining if a person is nervous or has some medical condition. Perhaps you will save yourself some heartache, since the other party may have a good reason to be nervous if he is planning something from which you will suffer!

Posture. Observe how a person carries himself. There is a difference between the erect bearing of the career officer or noncom and the calculated slouch of the equally dedicated dropout. The depressed or discouraged person will portray a message with the shoulders drawn together and the back hunched forward. The high head and springy step of the lover offers a different feeling. The potbelly, lacking any tone, of the elderly or lazy person bespeaks a lack of value placed upon health and vigor. At one time it was considered a measure of one's worldly success to be fat. Today flabbiness points to one's giving up the values of health and beauty. Such a person may have some other values, but self-esteem is lacking. The wariness of some, the indifference of others, the tension of many are all revealed in posture.

Our identity is established in the eyes of others through our *manner or style* as well as what we say. For some people, style is all. Others prefer an unadorned simplicity.

We display in our *dress* to some extent the picture that we have of ourselves, our values, and also the picture which we wish to portray to others. The woman who wears the latest Fifth Avenue fashion and hairstyle appears different from one who wears faded jeans and cropped hair. Both of these women have a different self-image from the obese woman wearing a shapeless dress.

Social roles also tell us how a person wants to be regarded. There are plenty of familiar examples, i.e., the "vamp" or seductress, the "cavalier," the "Southern belle," etc.

The unconscious level of expression. This has been left till last for good reason. It is difficult to understand, though it affects many aspects of behavior. Therefore, I want to give you some awareness of the general complexity of people's reactions before exposing you to the most perplexing hidden factor of all. The unconscious means a way of reacting to life whose meaning is self-concealed. This does not mean that others cannot make accurate estimates of the meaning of your words and actions, only that they are not clear to you yourself. Ideas, feelings, and action-tendencies often become unconscious because of anxiety. Repression, or the creation of unconscious meanings, comes from the childhood experience of disapproval by parents and others. Such feelings as sexual desire, anger, and dependency may not have been permitted or might have resulted in punishment. However, emotionally brutalizing parents cannot destroy basic human nature. They can only cause us to hide our real needs. Thus, a person may deny being hostile, but his posture, the way he treats his family and subordinates, an occasional slip of the tongue, may indicate a buried anger which he is now *displacing* to others. Similarly with sex. A woman might claim that she has no sexual desire, or that her husband completely satisfies her. Closer examination might show seductive postures, provocative reading matter, revealing clothing, and an excessive interest in the sexual development of her children. A child can be taught he must rely only on himself and to believe that others are not giving and warm. Thus he may be trained not to show his dependency. The relationships he forms could be demanding, filled with frustration and anger because what is expected is excessive. Yet he might not be aware of the depth of his needs.

Let me warn you, however. Do not be an amateur psychologist! It is far better to insist that people treat you with dignity, respecting your own needs (maybe even unconscious ones), than to try to analyze the unconscious of the next person. Even the pros can make mistakes.

THE SOCIAL RELATIONSHIP SELF-INTERVIEW

How about some practical experience in evaluating your social relationships? Are you ready to consider intensively the nature of your relationship with somebody important? Aw, go ahead. Think of somebody important to you. Now, interview yourself, using this person as the subject of these questions.

1. How do I feel?
2. Am I satisfied with the way I am treated?
3. Am I able to, or encouraged to, pursue my goals?
4. Are our lifestyles consistent, including the mutual degree of commitment?
5. Are our values consistent?
6. Am I free to feel, act, talk the way I want to?
7. Do we respect each other?
8. Is criticism moderate and constructive, or irrational, harsh, and excessive?
9. Are we transferring feelings from other relationships to this relationship?
10. Is either of us in this relationship only because loneliness is terrible?
11. Do I have other resources?
12. When we become angry, do we resolve our problems, ignore them, or make them worse?
13. Do I live for my needs, the other person's needs, or both?
14. How does my partner treat other people?
15. Is my partner consistent in what he/she says and does?
16. Is he/she telling the truth or lying?
17. Does my partner express feelings, attitudes, intentions, and goals?
18. Is my partner supportive in time of difficulty?
19. Does my partner take initiative in proposing activities?
20. Does my partner take some responsibility in terms of money, problem-solving, domestic responsibilities?
21. Do both of us show an active interest in each other's welfare?
22. Does either or both of us put up barriers to the expression of intimacy?
23. Is there a feeling of trust, i.e., that we are safe and treated with good faith?

8) Coping with Emotional Pain

By this time you have made a self-evaluation of your emotional discomforts and of the stresses in your life. You are now ready to begin the task of reducing self-destructiveness and increasing your emotional common sense.

Emotional pain, humiliation, and vulnerability are the key to many of your most unhappy hours and days. It is not only urgent that you recognize these feelings in yourself but imperative, indeed justified, that you express them. There is as much damage done to people by stifling their hurt feelings as there is in forbidding their sexuality and preventing their self-assertion.

I define *pain inhibition* as the inability to express hurt feelings in social relationships, with the intention of improving the relationship subsequent to the encounter. (Much of the subsequent discussion is based on the article "The Patient Who Cannot Express Pain," by R. S. Parker in the book *The Emotional Stress of War, Violence, and Peace*, 1972.) You can recognize that you suffer from pain inhibition if you have some of the following reactions: diminished sense of self-respect, frequent depressions, feelings of shame, inability to assert yourself, detachment, social anxieties, holding back anger until you are in a rage, inability to express love or to ask for emotional support, and proneness to feel exploited by others. If you suffer from these symptoms, you are in serious trouble, because you have not learned how to defend yourself from destructive people.

It is important that you understand the relationship between pain and anger. Some people assert that anger is a primary feeling. When we are attacked in some way we get angry. Obviously, this is a marvelously true statement for a carnivore such as a lion or even for an elasmobranch such as a shark. However it is an inaccurate simplification for a complex mentality such as yours. Your self-concept conjures up a variety of feelings and symbolic meanings when events that are relevant to it occur. Sometimes it is involved even when no activity is really related to it. If you perceive the actions of another as damaging to your self-esteem or best interests, then you are likely first to experience emotional pain or humiliation. Then, and only then, unless you are a shark, you become angry. Let me repeat: Pain precedes anger. Since by now you are a sophisticated student of human nature, you wisely ask why it is that you may get angry but are not aware of the pain that preceded it. The reason is simply this: Many households and many influences in our culture discourage the expression of pain (and also of anger). What seems to happen is that, first, the communication of emotional pain is held back. Then the actual feeling is inhibited. Thus some people may not be aware that unconsciously they feel humiliated, tormented, or abused.

Emotional pain or humiliation is experienced by people who feel vulnerable or sensitive. While it is possible to describe some people as being excessively sensitive, most people are trained not to show their pain, regardless of its extent. This is the epitome of self-destructiveness, since it gives others a hunting license with us as a target. More about this later. The basis for emotional pain is the experience of being treated with disdain when one is a child. The child who is respected by his or her parents, who is not overwhelmed with criticism or punishment, grows up with a sense of personal value which is not easily disturbed. Often enough the vulnerable person had his self-esteem rendered fragile by parents who, as victims of parental abuse themselves and suffering from feelings of inadequacy, turned around and bullied their own children. How often does a parent degrade a child's best efforts? Perhaps this disapproval is indirect—for example, expecting perfection, so that even good effort is treated as being inadequate. Another favorite way of manipulating a child is through provoking guilt. I had a fifty-year-old patient who insisted that he would be the death of his still-alive eighty-five-year-old mother. Playing favorites of one child over another makes the rejected child feel valueless and angry. Sometimes a child is mercilessly compared to others: Their achievement is much better than yours. Another route to vulnerability is to be bullied by neighborhood toughs without parental solace or protection.

When children are threatened, they object, they cry, they retreat, or ultimately they may withdraw. All these are cues to observant and caring parents that their children's feelings are hurt, that they are overwhelmed by stronger forces, that their growing egos are being misshapen and left with wounds, scars, and defenseless areas. The sensitive parent will then try to make amends or to change. Perhaps to undo the damage, the child will be sent to psychotherapy and the parents will participate in counseling.

Sometimes parents are motivated to teach the child not to express his pain in order to keep themselves from feeling guilty and to keep the child as a target to enable themselves to feel superior.

The emphasis I place upon the role of pain inhibition in self-destructive behavior can be observed from the fact that this is our first chapter on coping with specific problem areas. I want you to be able to recognize it in yourself and to avoid inflicting it on your children. After we see some of the symptoms of pain inhibition, I will show you some of the specific ways in which parents teach their children not to annoy them by showing their feelings. Then you will learn how to cope with the emotional pain that you may experience.

The social relationships of people who do not experience or express their pain have definite self-destructive characteristics. It must be remembered that neither pain nor anger goes away. They build up and may be expressed suddenly, excessively, and against the wrong target on unpredictable occasions. What often happens is that the pain-inhibiting adult, probably just like yourself, builds up anger and finally, when "the last straw breaks the camel's back," has an outburst of rage and hopelessly ruins a relationship or continues in an overly sensitive, inflamed mood. Relationships where one person inflicts pain and another inhibits it are filled with resentment. The destructive experience does not change. Sometimes the situation is made even worse by the pain inhibitor's refusal or inability to express his feelings. Sometimes it is experienced as frustrating when one party does not express his feelings. Perhaps the passivity is considered to be an invitation to continue the abuse, or that this torment is likely to be continued.

Feelings are a signal that important events are taking place. It is meaningless to ask whether feelings offer rational information, because rationality implies a different phase of experience. It is more meaningful to ask, What are the events that stirred up the feelings? What are the feelings like? Have we properly interpreted what is happening to us? Which actions will be consistent with our welfare and which will be self-destructive?

HOW HOMES SHAPE EMOTIONAL LIFE

At this point it will be useful to study home influences which encourage the emotional crippling I have described as *pain inhibition* (Parker, 1972b). Households can be described as being *expressive, nice, abusive, emotionally depriving,* and *guilt-provoking*—or some combination of these.

The "expressive" household. Feelings are encouraged as legitimate, and the child's ego is built up because he is treated as a valuable individual. The parents *educate the child concerning the language of the emotions.* They teach him/her that certain kinds of feelings occur when people are treated one way or another, explain the reactions of people to particular events in the child's life, explain their own feelings and express them in a way that is not excessively punitive. They don't prevent the child from reacting with his own feelings. In short, they help the child to understand his own reactions.

The "nice" household. The expression of strong feelings such as pain and anger is discouraged. Children are taught to value propriety and the illusion of good will over the reality of experiencing this world as unreasonable, frustrating, provoking, depriving, and sexual. There are specific *ideologies* which express strength and discourage weakness. It might be considered more important to express love or charity or to live in a genteel way, than to experience or recognize such a basic feeling as personal pain. Perhaps the child is taught that the only way to have self-respect is to conceal pain and weakness. Such precepts are offered as "Don't be a crybaby"; "Don't show others your weakness or they will take advantage of you"; "Keep a stiff upper lip"; and other drivel. The parents' hidden agenda is that the respect of society, neighbors, and relatives is more important to them than the child's feelings; the hidden command is "Be nice so that everybody will think that we are great parents." The effects of this upbringing may be found in Chekhov's *Three Sisters*. Roger Garris' *New York Times* review (8/10/69) made the point admirably. "It is a play about the consequences of living by a certain code of courtesy, taste and gentility. . . . The dark underside of the sisters' hypersensitivity about other people's manners is their trained incapacity to recognize other people's violent impulses and intentions."

The "abusive" home. Here you learn that the best way to solve a problem is with a loud voice, short temper, a slap, or an exaggerated insult. The child finds that good human relationships result from verbal or physical assaults. Through *survival of the nastiest*, the correct emotional atmosphere will evolve in which all parties can figure out how to work together harmoniously. In this atmosphere, anger and pain are magnified because of personal experience, or the model of the parents. Physical and verbal abuse results from opposition to them. Resentment causes punishment. The model that the parents create has further self-destructive effects. If the child identifies with the passive victim, he may become incapacitated by a feeling of helplessness before aggressors, accompanied by contempt for the victim (his parent), and ultimately by a feeling of detachment from people. As an adult, when he is attacked his defenses are hampered, and finally after a period of attack he experiences waves of destructive anger or crippling fear. Furthermore, brutal parents create brutal children. One man I know, who committed rape and many other atrocities against prisoners of war, had refused as a boy to give his father the satisfaction of expressing pain, although he was frequently beaten into unconsciousness. His motto was "No matter how much you hurt me, I don't cry."

When a person reared in an "abusive" household forms a relationship with someone from a different background, the latter never knows what hit him. Fortunate is the one who discovers early in a relationship that the fighting style of his mate is to meet the slightest challenge with the emotional equivalent of an uppercut.

The "emotionally depriving" home. The parents are

basically unreactive because they don't want to have the responsibility of emotional involvement. The child's warmth, frustration, love, anger, and manipulations are ignored. He learns that his feelings are of no value in influencing others. He experiences rejection, and ultimately turns off his feelings in order to spare himself the humiliation of being emotionally ignored. *"It does no good to express hurt feelings; in fact it would make matters worse."* Some parents are downright exploitative, depriving their children of medical attention, sacrificing one child to another, putting their own desires above the legitimate ones of their children, infantilizing the child to keep him around, or using him for their own ego trips. Above all, the child must not raise anxiety concerning their weaknesses, neuroses, and hypocrisy.

Some unresponsive parents are incapable of expressing, or choose not to express, their feelings toward their children. Consequently, the child never learns to properly evaluate the feelings of others, since his parents did not accompany their actions with explanations of feelings. When people grow up in such a household, they learn to value being "cool," i.e., nonresponsive and detached. They frustrate someone who wants a lively interchange, whether loving or fighting. In fact, if you really want to be self-destructive, be persistent in engaging such a withdrawn person in a love affair!

The "guilt-provoking" household. The child is kept in line by predicting dire consequences, such as the death of the parents or the criticism of the neighbors. People raised in such households often enter into sado-masochistic relationships with hostile, punishing partners who create resentment and anger. These create on the one hand punishment for old-time feelings of guilt, and on the other the hope (generally frustrated) of being vindicated for the years of being told that one was a terrible kid. One partner abuses the other in the hope of finally being punished sufficiently to alleviate neurotic guilt, while the other hopes to convert this wretch into the loving parent he/she cared for years before.

DEALING WITH EMOTIONAL PAIN

The first step in handling emotional pain is to *recognize* it. Become sensitive to the connection between social events and your feelings. You will be able to label those feelings which accompany abrasive situations as painful, humiliating, and so on.

The next step I call the "ouch principle." It is so simple that you will be immediately ashamed that you did not discover it yourself. When somebody steps on your toes, say, "Ouch!" Or, "You have hurt my feelings," or, "I don't like the way I am being treated." It is truly amazing to consider the vast number of people who violate the "ouch principle." I became particularly aware of this when I suggested to one of my therapy groups that people can be divided into those who elevate and those who depress one's spirits. The look of enlightenment and happiness that they expressed told me that the group members understood this simple description of human interaction as being very valuable.

Watch the reaction of the other person. Some people will be genuinely chagrined that they have offended you. They will express their concern. Value them. Others will try to explain why they have acted the way they did. It may be that there was a misunderstanding, that they did not mean to be offensive, or perhaps their criticism was justified and you are genuinely oversensitive. In this case, the relationship can also be maintained through the interchange of honest feelings.

There are others whose emotional reactions to being told that they have hurt your feelings will be quite different. They will deny it or accuse you of being overly sensitive. They will maintain that they have a right to their opinion. Perhaps they will try to hurt you again because they have found a weak spot. The only way that you can identify these vicious people is to take a risk by expressing your feelings. It ought not to be hard to separate those individuals who are emotionally expressive without intending to downgrade you from those who will continue to do so regardless of how you feel.

Eliminate resolutely from your life those people who are indifferent or hurtful to your feelings. There is nothing in your experience that is more important than your feelings. Generally, almost any kind of hardship can be borne with decent grace if one's self-respect can be maintained. It is self-destructive to associate with so-called friends, abusive employers, mean spouses or abusive offspring if there is any alternative. I repeat:

The most satisfactory way of coping with emotional pain is to identify and seek out those people who elevate your spirits and avoid those who depress them. I have done this myself after the most serious crisis of my own life and have never regretted it. It is self-destructive to be gnawed away at in the name of friendship, loyalty, family, and other distractions. It is emotional common sense to surround yourself with those who value you, who try to make you feel good, who forgive you your faults, who support you when the going is rough.

Since you may be sufficiently self-destructive not to take this emotional common sense at its face value, let me take up some objections which have been made to it. One person accused me of instigating guilt-provoking behavior. If by this is meant to prey on others' weaknesses, I say this is ridiculous. In the first place, many people who provoke hurt feelings really are guilty of emotional or physical brutality. Secondly, such opponents of pain expression believe that one should defend oneself through the immediate, direct expression of anger. This is particularly destructive. There is already a vast amount of unreasoned anger in the world. By expressing pain early in a relationship, before serious anger develops, the victim has a number of options. He can explain his position, inquire into the feelings of the other person, be angry, leave, and so forth. He does not immediately provoke a fight and thus risk making the situation immediately worse.

There are ways of protecting oneself which do make the situation worse. There is a difference between saying, "You hurt my feelings," and making an accusation. "I feel humiliated" brings out one response from a person, and "You are a son of a bitch" brings out another. It is generally wiser to express your own feelings first and then later, if the situation warrants, to point out the inadequacies of the other. The latter step, unless tactfully handled, may be experienced as a provocation for a fight or the end of a relationship. Unless you mean either of these, proceed with caution.

What about the question of revealing your vulnerability? It is quite likely that your overly sensitive areas have already been targeted by your opponent, so the risk of further damage to your ego is minimal. The benefits from expressing your hurt are maximal, since you can clearly identify friends from foes.

Think of the soldier who raises his helmet on a stick to see if it will be fired on!

One reason that is frequently given for staying in an abusive relationship is the fear of loneliness. "If I don't accept the pain, there is the greater pain of eternal loneliness." Let me state quite categorically: Get rid of the pain-provoking person, then you will have the time and good spirits to find someone who will value and care for you and stir up warmth and love. It is also most important that you develop other resources which will occupy your time and enhance your self-esteem.

How about my grown children? One of the most frequent complaints I have heard involves humiliation and hostility from one's children. This creates moral conflicts, since love and caring are probably built into our genes and reinforced through social pressure. Nevertheless, there is no question that parents suffer from hostility and degrading actions from their children. I have personally known many people whom I liked and respected as parents who have told me of being mistreated. They felt that it was their duty to continue to be devoted and loving. Inwardly, they probably felt that they were miserable failures as parents and were perplexed by this.

It was never easy to be a good parent, but the current social structure has made it even more difficult. When I was growing up, the older generation represented a kind of compass point. One might aspire to be like them or rebel against them, but the adult world was the framework into which one was moving. Children who have grown up more recently have been molded by different experiences and values. Mobility makes it easy to leave home early and travel large distances. Affluence creates demands first and then boredom. The media (TV, records, radio, press) are either new or more available, and have been shaped for commercial reasons by exploitative persons who have created a "youth culture." This emphasizes immediate gratification and a demand for high levels of stimulation. Youth have been influenced simultaneously by these products and each other more than by parents, teachers, and clergy. Thus the "generation gap" is greater than it has been, because of different expectations, influences, and freedoms. Whether parents have been conservative or liberal in raising their children, young people have been trained to react more easily to frustration, with freedom to express harsh feelings.

If you have been mistreated (according to your lights) by your children, I believe that the same principles hold as in other relationships. Try to settle the problems in a mutually respectful way. Look within. It is possible that some of their resentments of you are deserved. It is possible that in your present relationship with your children you have been patronizing or critical. If so, then it is your responsibility to treat them as adults, i.e., responsible people with their own values and goals. Should it be that the resentments are ancient history, then you might ask them to live in the present and to build a new kind of bond. Yet, if the pattern of hostility continues, what is your obligation? Emotional common sense says that when your children are grown you have completed your duties and are free to lead your own life, to seek your own fulfillment. Call those rotten kids in, and say, "Goodbye. I have better things to do than be abused. Drop me a postcard in ten years if you're still alive." The great genius Ludwig von Beethoven wrote to his nephew Karl, in 1825: "God is my witness, I dream only of one thing, to be entirely rid of you and this wretched brother of mine and this abominable family which has been foisted upon me. May God grant my wishes, for never again shall I be capable of suffering on your account."*

Beethoven: Letters, Journals and Conversations (Michael Hamburger, translator and editor). Garden City, N.Y.: Anchor Books, 1960, p. 235.

9) Alleviating Guilt, Shame and Unreal Obligations

The painful feelings treated in this chapter are further proof of the harmfulness of the dictum that "You must always trust your feelings." One of the swiftest throughways on the route to self-destructiveness is to make decisions on the basis of being an inferior, wrongdoing person.

I am not stating that "anything goes" in human relations, so that no matter what we do to others we ought to be free of guilt. People are vulnerable, and the aftereffects of bad treatment can be extensive and long-lasting. Consequently, so many of us who are basically decent, productive, and considerate of others' feelings travel through life as though we were sinners about to be condemned to one of Dante's circles in the *Inferno*: "I entered on the roadway deep and wild and saw these words inscribed upon a rock: Through me lies the road to the city of grief: Through me lies the pathway to woe everlasting: Through me lies the road to the souls that are lost. . . . Abandon hope, all ye who enter here!" *

As we grow up there are a variety of ways in which we learn how to measure our virtue and worthiness.

• *Super-ego*—our conscience. When we think that we do something wrong, then we feel *guilty*.

• *Ego-ideal*—our model for perfection. When we deviate below some great standard, we feel *shame* (Helen Block Lewis, 1971).

• *Obligations*—what we must do to make people around us

*Cantos 2, 3, translated by Lawrence Grant White.

happy and earn their praise. When we don't do what is expected of us we feel *unworthy and disappointing.*

Super-ego, ego-ideal, and obligations are "identification nuclei" which shape our behavior and moods by creating rewards and criticism. At the same time, we are given moral instructions. The earliest examples might be toilet training and the prohibition against masturbation. These are strictly personal functions, but compliance is compulsory. Later on, as we become more socialized, there develops a demand for socially valuable performances, e.g., being polite, doing well in school, excelling in sports or dancing or sewing. Some parents feel guilty when there is something emotionally wrong with the child. Others identify with the child and feel unworthy if their child is not successful. In many ways, parents pressure a child to meet their expectations. They enforce conformity with punishment, criticism, withdrawal of love, adverse comparisons with others, and similar advanced educational practices. Indeed it is not even permitted to be unhappy, because this means that the parents are rotten, i.e., they haven't produced a happy child. Some parents give their children double messages: "Don't do this, yet I expect you to do it because I did it myself" (Furman, 1979).

GUILT

Our super-ego consists of the moral instructions that have been set for us so that we can impress family, educators, and society as good people. Violation of the moral code causes us to feel "guilty." At first the accusation comes from some friendly authority. After a while we accent it. We observe ourselves, and when we commit some violation we accuse ourselves and experience guilt, depression, humiliation, low self-esteem, and dread.

The self-accusation can be far too severe for the transgression. Consequently, there are terrible feelings of unworthiness. Frequently the pain resulting from the self-accusation is so great that we bury it, i.e., it becomes repressed ("*unconscious guilt*").

Neurotic guilt contributes to destructive relationships, such as sado-masochism, where the aggressor tries to provoke the willing victim into punishing him for old-time violations. Guilt also creates other distortions in emotional life and relationships.

Let's look at Mary, a young woman in her twenties who is constantly angry with her roommate, Julia. Julia pouts and cries when Mary has a date, because she can't stand being alone. However, if Mary takes her along, she cannot decide what restaurant to go to. When Mary leaves her at home, she injures herself, perhaps while cooking. Mary feels guilty because she won't spend much time with Julia now that there is a new man in her life. I asked her why she was so reluctant to show her anger. She told me that when she was a girl, and her friends would make her angry, she would scratch them and pull their hair. Then she would feel terrible. She still cannot confront people, because this means being angry, which would make her feel like a bad person. She felt better after speaking about her anger, and being told that anger was a legitimate feeling.

Let us look at the guilty or valueless person, perhaps you yourself. The deepest feelings of sex or anger are forbidden. Meeting new people or dealing as an equal with those you now know becomes a strain: "They cannot accept me. I cannot be myself. I cannot be happy with others. I must reproach myself for being a human being with all of the drives and temptations. I must avoid deep relationships. I must keep people from stirring up my feelings. I must not talk to that attractive stranger, because he will reject me. I must not change jobs, because no other person will hire me. I cannot have a restful moment, because I think of my sins."

There are a variety of disastrous effects of feeling guilt-ridden and thus valueless. Consider the need for approval. Relationships are formed and activities are directed not toward obtaining pleasure but rather to satisfy the need to be liked, of being told that you are good. This is an extreme form of dependency. Thus, while some people restrict their feelings and relationships because they are guilty, others must alleviate their sense of guilt through always giving to others, and pleasing them.

Another unfortunate result of having a guilty conscience is either to accept abuse or even to provoke it. There are plenty of people in this life whose displaced hostilities, arrogance, and tortured self-esteem cause them to try to feel better at the expense of brutalizing others. They are looking for targets and you will do nicely. If you believe that you are a moral failure, that you do not deserve good treatment, that you are not a valuable, useful human being, then you will stand by and let yourself be further brutalized. You will continue to feel like a worthless piece of trash. Perhaps you will let others increase your belief that you are evil and condemned.

Some individuals actually provoke punishment or rejection. You must be sensitive to this in yourself or others. Do not play this game. One of the consequences of being treated like a guilty child is to believe you are one and then to try to alleviate this supreme sense of discomfort. Since we have a defective brain, instead of building up our ego through acts of love and productivity we accept the neurotic symptom. Individuals can provoke the anger of others or society's institutionalized punishment in order to be punished and thus relieved of their guilt. This is a telling argument against capital punishment, i.e., some people will murder in order to be executed themselves. However, this is a complex problem.

Some act in an irritating way in order to be rejected. They seem to feel more comfortable with the idea that they are valueless. They must prove that they are not lovable. This is ridiculous, you say. Why would people do things so self-destructive as to provoke others to reject them, to reduce their self-esteem further? Sometimes the alternative is for these people to admit that they are worthwhile. But if they are worthwhile, then those who mistreated them, who told them that they were no good, were themselves evil or rotten people. We are so conditioned to assume that our parents or other authorities are right and we are wrong that we sometimes don't consider this possibility. We would feel guilty if we said to our parents, "You are mistreating me. Your values are wrong, your opinions misguided, your experience narrow. You lack a willingness to let me grow up and be my own person. You are not emotionally giving, loving, encouraging, supporting." To avoid this emotionally shattering conclusion, the person would rather provoke rejection, because to be accepted would be to prove that he is not guilty, not dirty, and not evil; rather he was mistreated by someone he loved.

How can you recognize this attitude in yourself? Here is how some people verbalize it:

- "I never felt that I deserved anything."
- "I am not deserving or entitled."
- "I expected all supervisors to be authoritarian and beat me down."
- "If I don't accept the pain, there is the greater pain of loneliness."
- "I cry when I feel helpless and out of control."

Another consequence of guilt is being susceptible to emotional blackmail and guilt-provocation. If we doubt our basic morality, then we are the target of hostile, exploitative people who will use us for their own purposes. Emotional blackmail is the threat to become angry or be unpleasant if the target does not act the way the blackmailer desires. "If you object to the way I treat you, then I will kick, scream, have a tantrum, embarrass you, and in other ways cause you to act the way I want you to." Guilt-provocation is an equally insidious form of manipulation, implying that the other party is going to cause extreme pain, is a sinner, is a bad person. Emotional common sense dictates that after we understand our motives, if we feel that they are genuine and not designed to exploit others, then we resolutely tell these people that we will be the guide of our own actions and will not be affected by their concepts of how we should act. They are entitled to lead their own lives, but will have to pay the consequences for the way in which they treat us.

SHAME

We can think of our super-ego as a set of standards we set for ourselves as what not to do (conscience). Our ego-ideal, on the other hand, informs us as to what kind of behavior is valuable. To be a crook is to do something active. This violates our conscience. Not to be worthwhile, however, is a deviation from the standard of being a valuable public citizen. When we tell ourselves that our heroes were all pure, brave, intelligent, attractive, and shrewd, it is easy to fall from grace. If we are very sensitive, then to experience ourselves as not having lived up to our own expectations, even though they may have been learned from others, is to experience shame and humiliation. As psychologist H. Heckausen put it (see Helen B. Lewis, 1971, p. 121), even children of three and a half know the difference between personal failure (shame) and task failure (ineptness). When we don't live up to the ideals of people we idealize, we lose love for ourselves. Consequently, we may feel that others will reject us and in turn become angry. Some of us then displace this anger into the destruction or humiliation of others (see Chapter 11). However, if a potential target is actually somebody we don't want to lose, we might turn the anger on ourselves, becoming depressed and suffering from feelings of valuelessness (Chapter 12).

Shame can sometimes be experienced as guilt. It can also be verbalized as a "*should*," directing us how to behave. A man said, "I felt guilty that the tenant upstairs from my mother hadn't paid her the rent by the twentieth of the month. I feel guilty when I don't take initiative." (I asked him where he got the obligation to take the initiative? Who told you that you were the kind of kid that doesn't take initiative?) "I used to be told that. I still get told that. My mother starts mumbling that the person upstairs hasn't paid the rent. I should say something to her. She tells me I let people get away with things. I can see my own role. Why am I so hesitant to ask the person for money?" (I should be able to spare my mother this unpleasant task.)

UNREAL OBLIGATIONS

Unreal obligations arise from the various "shoulds" we accumulate. I define an unreal obligation as a moral pressure to do something excessive or not necessary. So what does excessive mean? What is gained in exchange for the service is minimal, because emotional blackmail maintains the feeling of obligation by threat of loss of love, playing upon the victim's vulnerability, pretending to be more helpless than the facts justify, provoking guilt to keep up the service. The victim says, "I should do this because I will feel guilty if I don't, since the person I serve will fall apart/drop dead/hate me/won't love me/once did something for me.

A woman consulted with me because she was unable to cope with the thought of being transferred to a job working for a difficult female supervisor. We reviewed her work with another psychotherapist. She said that, when she wasn't getting any-place with him, "He gave me the feeling that I wasn't making progress by taking the next step." (I commented to her that she was a pretty reprehensible kid.) "My mother told me, 'You're a schlemiel. You can't do anything right. You're like your father. If you listen to Mommy, you'll be OK, otherwise you won't make it in the world.' She thought I was a nothing." ("You couldn't satisfy your mother, you couldn't make her happy.") "I was a good student." ("You couldn't satisfy your mother," I repeated.) "Why couldn't she be happy with me?" ("What was your role in life?") "To make my mother happy." ("Do you think that you can face your new supervisor?") "It makes me angry to face my mother again. The dissatisfied woman. I never succeeded in satisfying her, during all my growing years. My new boss is not an easy person to satisfy."

Her obligation is to please her mother and make her happy, otherwise she is guilty and anxious.

MORALITY AND EMOTIONAL COMMON SENSE

Questions of morality are generally related to early training. It is true that some people may have a profound change in their values during maturity, but that is generally under the impact of new, disturbing situations with which the old attitudes could not cope. As part of our maturation, we develop some attitudes concerning what standards we should accept. Familiar examples are the variety of religious codes; but as if this were not enough, there are many family credos which are based on the peculiarities of the idiots who teach them. I had a patient who was taught by his grandfather that "people are either steel to be hammered, or the anvils upon which they are shaped." As a result, he thought that all human relationships involved the sense of power, and he himself felt constantly "shaped" by others and thus powerless.

Moral codes involve, of course, how we should act. But after all, actions are generally directed at particular people or groups of people. Any standard of behavior or moral code, then, has to affect our human relationships. We may have been shaped by eternal fire and brimstone, by fear of rejection or isolation, by condemnation, or by public scorn. In addition to the fear of what people will say about us and the consequences of a little passion or anger (guilt), we can also develop a sense that our entire person is valueless (low self-esteem). We learn that what we have done condemns us as entire personalities.

As we learn the standards of our parents, religious authorities, neighbors, teachers, and other influential personalities, we may learn ways to behave which enhance our individuality or provide useful guides to action in the real world. On the other hand, we may have to deny our very flesh, our capacity to love ourselves or others, the power to defend ourselves. We may have to give up our peace of mind, our sense of being valuable people, our hope of some eternal peace and rest after death. All this martyrdom at the insistence of some people who demand compliance with their own standards of value, without caring about the emotional consequences to the person they are guiding.

I am certainly not advocating the abolition of all standards of behavior and morality. However, even a casual look at the way people treat one another in the world will be strong evidence that the current moral standards have given justification for vast amounts of emotional and physical destruction.

A NEW SENSE OF VALUES

These new values may be within organized institutions, or they may represent those of people you esteem or perhaps a new creation which meets the test of your personal experiences. Many people change their confessors, stop visiting their guilt-provoking parents, join new religious denominations, or read extensively in philosophy. The important thing is to expose yourself to new values and ideas.

Learn to recognize the particular situations which provoke emotional discomfort in you or which play on your inadequacies. You may discover that particular people or classes of people or certain kinds of situations or locations make you anxious, guilty, or inadequate. Try to associate these experiences with the original training that you had. Perhaps a certain teacher or supervisor reminds you of an earlier religious teacher or parent. Perhaps somebody stirs up a sexual or anger impulse. Tell yourself that you will live in the present. Evaluate every situation in terms of what it means for your present satisfaction or the realistic consequences. Anxiety and the rest of your emotional discomforts may be an unrealistic forecast of what will happen if you do what you feel like doing.

Temporarily disregard your feelings. Tell yourself that the feeling of guilt or anxiety or valuelessness is irrational. I am not saying that your emotional discomfort will rapidly or automatically disappear. Rather, by ceasing to restrict your activities you will have the opportunity to engage in new experiences, to test and learn new values, to meet new people, and basically to experience yourself differently. Above all, give up the idea that any failure is the beginning of a string of failures or of disaster.

What if your anxiety and guilt are based on a realistic estimate of your treatment of others and how they feel about you? It should be obvious that to destroy the well-being of others has been self-destructive from your own point of view. If you don't give a damn about the feelings of others, this book isn't meant for you anyway.

10) Relieving Anxiety and Tension

Anxiety and tension rank among the most uncomfortable and disabling emotions. They are hard to understand and cope with because their source is frequently only indirectly associated with today's events. People differ considerably from birth in their feeling of vulnerability, i.e., their readiness to feel nervous. There is even a new specialty called "infant psychiatry." The same experiences have effects that differ not only in their initial intensity but also in the period of time that the stress reaction lasts.

The unpleasant, even catastrophic, moods of anxiety and tension can be experienced cognitively (i.e., in a belief that some catastrophe is likely to strike) or in somatic symptoms (e.g., palpitations and other cardiac symptoms that can mimic a heart attack; sweating, trembling, diarrhea, rapid breathing [hyperventilation], muscular tension, paleness, dryness of the mouth). Anxiety is maintained by brain circuits and neurotransmitters that stimulate the body in a variety of ways. Therefore it may be faster to deal directly with the feelings of discomfort than to try to unravel our childhood neuroses. However, while relief of anxiety contributes to our happiness and efficiency, its origins and effects could still hamper our creativity and our ability to choose a suitable mate or career.

How prevalent is anxiety? According to Tallman et al. (1980), in 1977 in the U.S. at least 8,000 tons of the milder tranquilizers (benzodiazepines) were consumed. These included 54 million prescriptions for Valium and 13 million for Librium.

PSYCHOLOGICAL ORIGINS OF ANXIETY

The initial cause of anxiety is separation from one's mother or other caretaker. On a temporary basis this is terrible enough for the child. However, when a child is separated unwillingly from his mother, and placed in a strange environment, a number of events take place which are the precursors of a variety of later emotional difficulties (Bowlby, 1973).

First, the child *protests* vigorously. This is the beginning of a potential for *separation anxiety.*

Second, the child seems to *despair of recovering the mother,* though he remains preoccupied with her and vigilant in the hope of her return. This anticipates grief and mourning.

Finally, the child loses his interest and becomes *emotionally detached, i.e., defended against having close relationships.*

Why should the mind create this enormous vulnerability? After all, these were findings from children who were well taken care of, i.e., sufficiently to survive and grow up. In fact, Bowlby suggests that it is natural to have many fears. It is pathological *not* to be afraid of strangers, darkness, noises, and being alone (1973, p. 84).

The answer is that in our evolutionary past it was dangerous to leave the protection of your parents. You were likely to be a leopard's weekly minimum dietary allowance for protein. In another book, Bowlby (1969, p. 226) notes that anxiety in the absence of one's parents is a protection from predators by keeping the child close to home. This is as important as any other survival behavior. Also, when a child communicates fear and preference for his mother, this forms an alliance between mother and child (Emde, Gaensbauer, and Harmon, 1975, p. 122). However, reliance on a single caretaker creates a great vulnerability, and the effect is more devastating when that caretaker is lost or unable to meet the infant's needs. Moreover, situations that recreate separation anxiety are experienced as so threatening as to be overwhelming physiologically and psychologically.

MUSCULAR TENSION

One of the signs of anxiety is muscular tension. While sensing danger requires that we run or fight, in modern life we act as though there are brakes on our actions. Our muscles are generally in a state of restrained activity (tension). The importance of muscular tension in aggravating emotional disturbances—leading to psychosomatic illnesses and also aggravating any other illness—is detailed by Dr. Barbara Brown (1977), a leader in the study of biofeedback to reduce emotional distress. When we are in a state of alertness due to chronic danger, our muscles become tense, sleep is interfered with, and new anxiety brings the level of tension even higher. We become accustomed to the level of tension and are not aware of the destructive effects it has on us. Emotional tension, anticipation of difficulties, dreams, images of problems, all contribute to muscular tension.

Sigmund Freud (see particularly *Inhibitions, Symptoms, and Anxiety,* sometimes translated as *The Problem of Anxiety*) pointed out that anxiety takes many forms and that it is the basis for many of the major mental symptoms. It would be correct to state that many people's lives are organized to avoid anxiety or guilt, sometimes by extreme effort and distortions of their world. Freud recognized many forms of anxiety, including separation anxiety or fear of loss of the mother (we shall consider this in Chapter 14 on loneliness), danger from the external world (realistic anxiety), from the id (which becomes neurosis), and from the super-ego (the origin of guilt).

There are many familiar examples of *realistic anxiety,* such as the fear of a confrontation with a hoodlum on the street, or a narrow escape from a reckless driver while in a car, or of a truck careening down on us as we cross a road. This kind of anxiety is usually a correct signal that we are or have been in danger. Nevertheless, the way people handle realistic anxiety is often irrational. I myself did not learn to drive a car until I was twenty-six because of an excessive fear of being injured or of injuring others. Some people are reluctant to try new activities, because they were taught as children that the world is a very fearful place. As a result, travel, meeting new people, venturing into the streets at night, and so on become excessively troublesome to them. As two people put it, anxiety is "going through customs with three bottles," or even "going through customs with nothing to hide."

Other people take the opposite tack. They violate all common-sense precepts concerning their physical well-being. They court danger. Many examples come to mind: the girl who hitchhikes, the chronic speeder, the sky diver, the excessive smoker. On close observation these individuals are seen to be engaged in self-destruction. Many of them were fearful children and carry the illusion that they have to prove themselves to be adequate. Other individuals carry in their minds some false ideal as to the amount of daring or social revolt that is necessary for them to feel worthwhile. They imagine a crowd cheering them on or booing if they are "chicken," which is the real source of their daring. Their sense of valuelessness causes them to take the extreme position of conjuring up admirers and then performing for this hallucinated cheering section. Still others enter into what would ordinarily be anxiety-provoking situations because they are depressed and hopeless. They really want to die. They do not have the courage to take their life directly, so they hope that their misery will be alleviated through "an accident." Of course, they may end up maimed, or cause death and injury to others as well.

Thus, to give in needlessly to realistic anxiety means to restrict one's friends and activities and to reduce the possibility of achieving something worthwhile in the grand scale of one's life. On the other hand, to be daring or reckless may mean that one is engaged in activities which may have little value, or may only mean performing for some imaginary audience such as a gallery of relatives, neighborhood punks, and negativistic teachers who put you down unmercifully.

Neurotic anxiety is usually differentiated from fear because it does not seem to be directed toward any particular object. It is characterized by its pervasiveness and vagueness. It should be differentiated from a phobia, which is an unreasonable fear of a particular object or situation sufficiently intense to hamper a person's life.

How can you recognize if you suffer from neurotic anxiety? One answer is found in Henry Laughlin's The Neuroses (1967): "Anxiety may be regarded as pathologic when it is present to such an extent as to interfere with: (1) effectiveness in living, (2) the achievement of realistic goals or satisfactions, or (3) reasonable emotional comfort." Anxiety attacks are characterized by their suddenness, with both an emotional part (dread, apprehension, fear, terror) and a physiological reaction (heart palpitations, pain in the chest, fainting, cold hands or flushing, dizziness, numbness, perspiration, and disorders of the gastrointestinal tract, sexual organs, and neuromuscular systems). In fact, there are many serious medical problems which include the symptom of anxiety and a variety of specific medical conditions which either mimic it or bring on various symptoms similar to anxiety.

Emotional common sense, then, demands a vigorous attitude toward alleviating anxiety. First, it must be understood. Second, you must exercise self-discipline to unlearn old habits, and finally if these do not markedly reduce your discomfort, you should obtain whatever psychotherapeutic or medical assistance is necessary to bring your spirits back to well-being.

It is useful to understand anxiety in the light of both experience and heredity. It is likely that some people have a genetic disposition to experience new events with vulnerability, while others have the supreme gift of relative fearlessness. It has been extremely useful to me in my clinical practice to have my patients remember themselves as children or to ask their parents about their level of anxiety at an early age. Even well-meaning, non-neurotic parents can give birth to an anxious child. How they treat the child is another matter. The person who is anxious from birth, shows startle reactions and fear of strangers and may be more likely to attach his feelings to particular kinds of events, such as criticism, punishment, and fear of rejection.

Your experience of anxiety or the development of embarrassing, uncomfortable, or crippling emotional symptoms can be a result of what you have been trained to believe will be the consequences of your actions. If you were told that your father would cut your penis off if you masturbated, you are entitled to sexual anxiety. A girl may have been slapped by her mother when she caught her necking with the boy next door. All kinds of mistreatment are inflicted on children and youth for sexual activity. Similarly for anger. It is absolutely natural for children to be angry. Nevertheless, to react with anger may be an invitation to be hit, sent away from the table, screamed at, and deprived. As a result, when new situations arouse feelings of anger, the experience of anxiety arises for fear of the consequences.

Very often the actual situation that arouses anxiety is far removed from the original threat. There may be a recollection of somebody like the punishing parent; there may be a hostile or a sexually provocative person who stirs up our feelings. Perhaps there is a locale which reminds us of a deeply experienced sexual or hostile event in which we took part or for which we were punished. The result is the anxiety attack or the formation or increase of some symptoms. The trouble with symptoms is that they frequently represent not only the prevention of the drive and some emotional crippling, but unconsciously they also provide satisfaction, so that they are likely to be maintained. If one is prone to become anxious, a vague but distressing anxiety attack usually causes all other activities to cease while the individual struggles to regain his composure. The strength of the fear is measured by the fact that anxiety can be misinterpreted as a developing heart attack.

RELAXATION EXERCISES

These simple exercises have proven useful on many occasions in helping people who feel noticeably anxious, tense, or tired to feel much better. They are physiologically sound. Physicians (and drug companies) hate to see them in print because they are rapid and help people to avoid the use of medications or cut their use down.

Deep breathing. This exercise, when done correctly, is effective and can be practiced almost anywhere. You might try it before telling your boss what to do with his job, your girlfriend how you feel about her expensive habits, your husband about his indifference, and your parents about their sophisticated concepts of raising children!

1. Take a deep breath (you should *hear* yourself inhale)

2. Hold it (a few seconds)

3. Exhale hard (you should *hear* yourself exhale).

Repeat the sequence six times. Do not be afraid of excessive breathing (hyperventilation), because it is unlikely to occur. However, should you feel tingling in your fingers, that is a sign that you are in a stage of hyperventilation, and this exercise is to be avoided for the moment.

Stretching. These exercises are terrific when one is tense, and perhaps might help you go to sleep more easily. They are also fine at uncomfortable times during the day. The entire cycle occupies only one minute.

Stretching exercises are *not* intended to be a substitute for gymnastics. Do them comfortably. For example, deep knee bends can be done with a chair for support. Drooping (touch-toes) can be performed even with slightly bent knees. The important thing is that you become aware of the marvelous effects of stretching the overly tight muscles that fatigue you and create a distracting undercurrent of discomfort. Each phase is repeated a few times, and you might repeat the entire sequence more than once.

1. *Reach for the ceiling.* Stand on your toes, look upward, try to touch the ceiling.

2. *Rotate your head,* gently, to the left, to the right, upward, downward, in a circle, clockwise, and finally in a circle counterclockwise.

3. *Backstroke.* Hold your arms outstretched and rotate them backward, down, up, and around. Do it at a comfortable rate. The angle varies with how you feel, and how much constriction of motion there is due to tension and joint disease. Be gentle with yourself.

4. *Rotate your torso.* Hold your arms outstretched. Rotate your torso as far as it will go to the left, then to the right. Repeat a few times. The pace and extent of rotation vary according to how tight you are. As always, the important thing is to feel the lovely effect of stretching.

5. *Drooping.* Stand erect and gently let your torso droop forward until you can touch your toes, or as far as is comfortable. Just get the effect of stretching your back muscles and the long muscles of your legs. If you want to bend your knees, that is all right. Do not create any pain or have an exaggerated idea

as to how far down to go. It feels so good that it is habit-forming (maybe someday stretching will be illegal).

6. *Deep knee bends.* Stand erect and, either using a chair or un-supported, squat. Feel the stretching of tight muscles in the legs and seat. Repeat a few times—comfortably.

Progressive muscular relaxation. This is a great contribu-tion of Dr. Edmund Jacobson, though no doubt the system sug-gested here differs in some details. You will give yourself instructions to relax particular muscle groups. The entire proce-dure generally takes about fifteen minutes. However, I find that I can reduce headaches about 80 percent in a few minutes by applying a part of it, e.g., when I am in a public place. I just excuse myself, close my eyes, and relax the muscles in my head.

The beginning of this exercise involves getting familiar with the tightening and relaxation of your muscles.

I like to begin my progressive muscular relaxation with my clients by having them do the deep-breathing exercise (above).

- You might tell yourself to tighten and then relax: your jaws, your fists, your eyebrows.

- Then close your eyes and tell yourself to relax: your scalp—temples — forehead — eyebrows — eyelids — cheeks — lips — tongue—inside of your throat—back of your neck—shoulders.

- Then tell yourself that the relaxed feeling is traveling down your arms: past your upper arms—past your elbows—into your forearms—into your palms—into your thumb—second finger—third finger—fourth finger—little finger.

- Now the relaxed feeling is moving up your arms: past your el-bow—into your upper arms—into your neck—and shoulders.

- Now the relaxed feeling is going into your chest and into your abdomen: fill your abdomen with nice warm feelings—get rid of all the tension.

- Now the relaxed feeling is moving into your seat—into your hips—into your thighs—past your knees—into your calves—past your ankles—into your heels—into the balls of your feet.

- And now the relaxed feeling is moving into your big toe—into your second toe—third toe—fourth toe—and little toe.

If you wish, you can repeat the relaxation progression backward now, i.e., start it with your toes and work upward. You can end it with auto-suggestion (below) or use auto-suggestion separately.

Auto-suggestion. The following images can help you to relax or to fall asleep.

THE MEADOW. Imagine that you are lying down in the most comfortable meadow in the world. The sun is shining; it is very warm, but there is a marvelous breeze blowing. The grass is very soft, and you can smell it, and also some flowers. In the distance you can hear some birds. Imagine their song. Close by are some colored flowers. What color are they? Now a butterfly is coming close to you and is landing on one of your hands. You can feel the six little legs. What color is the butterfly? You can brush it off if you want to. As you add to the image, tell yourself that you are going into a deeper and more pleasant state of relaxation. Now imagine that all of the tension and anxiety remaining in your body is traveling into your abdomen. There is none left anywhere except in your belly. Now as you count from one to three, it will begin to leave your body and travel upward in the form of a colored cloud. As the cloud of tension leaves your body you will go into a deeper and more pleasant state of relaxation. What color is the cloud? Now the cloud is drifting upward, and as it goes higher and higher, you will go into a deeper state of relaxation. The cloud is now caught by the wind, and as it travels over the horizon you will be even more relaxed.

THE CLOUD. You are lying on the most beautiful and comfortable cloud in the world. It is very white. As you lie on the cloud, you are getting more and more relaxed. The sun is shining overhead, and the sky is very blue. Nearby, birds are flying by and you can hear their song. What kind of birds are they? As you lie on the cloud, feel the warm sun, see the blue sky, feel the cool breeze. You are going into a deeper and deeper state of relaxation. (Now see the image of the tension release from your abdomen from the previous auto-suggestion.)

Activity. There are some temporary measures which some people have found helpful while they are engaged in the long struggle against anxiety: calling friends to get a feeling of closeness; physical exercise; planning something to do for tomorrow;

typing; free associations until the unconscious meaning of the anxiety or guilt comes clear; reading poetry; listening to music and watching TV.

Finally, if you realize that anxiety, guilt, and valuelessness are an exaggerated reaction to old situations, that it is self-destructive to live in the past, then you can overcome these unhappy reactions and can face the future with a sense of well-being.

11) Reducing Interpersonal Antagonism

I approached the writing of this chapter with trepidation. Anger is so pervasive and people are so irrational in their selection of targets that it seems like a hopeless task to do something about it. Think of how unpredictable, unreasonable, and devious so many people are (including perhaps you, Gentle Reader, or me) in expressing aggression and hostility.

- They enjoy personal or institutionalized murder.
- They think nothing of hurting each other's feelings and are too proud to apologize.
- They try to justify the rottenest parts of human nature and action.

Do you believe that people are inherently good? This is nonsense propagated by foolish idealists. Seeing the world this way will prevent you from protecting yourself from sadistic creeps. Moreover, when you show some anger yourself, if you believe in inherent goodness you will unjustifiably abuse yourself for falling from grace.

It is human nature to be angry. People are not born good or bad, only infantile. Our early experience with our own anger and that of others shapes our personality. Anger—how we learn to cope with it and what makes us angry—has a bigger influence on who we become than sexual experiences. Consequently, it influences the way we cope with problems throughout our entire life. Indeed, the capacity for anger and rage is built into our nervous system (Elliott, 1976; Pinel, Treit, and Rovner, 1977; Mark and Ervin, 1970).

Since emotional common sense is a scientifically based approach to improving your emotional life, you must recognize that there is some controversy as to the very nature of human aggression. Famed sociobiologist Edmund O. Wilson asks rhetorically whether human beings are innately aggressive. "The answer is yes. Human forms of aggressive behavior contain features that distinguish them from aggression in all other species" (1978). Also: "It is hard to believe that any characteristic so widespread and easily invoked in a species as aggressive behavior in man could be neutral or negative in its effects on individual survival and reproduction" (1975, p. 265). Equally famed anthropologist Ashley Montagu (1977) disagrees: "If we truly understand the conditions that lead to aggressive behavior—and we believe them to be largely social—then we could bring about a virtual end to the expression of aggressive behavior in humans." Moreover, "Both the genetic determinance of aggression and its prehistoric practice have been greatly exaggerated ... human beings have lived rather more altruistically and peaceably over the greater part of their evolutionary history than well-known writers would have us believe" (1976, p. 9).

Your guide through the morass of your mind tends toward the former view, i.e., mankind (and the individual) doesn't take much stirring up to be pretty rotten. Biologist J. Z. Young (1978, p. 71) puts it nicely: "The capacity to throw tantrums is inborn," develops, and matures. There are inborn programs creating fear and anxiety which are reactions to possibly dangerous situations. These "prepare the individual to give an appropriately strong reaction of fight or flight" (p. 156).

EVOLUTIONARY ORIGINS OF AGGRESSION

Aggression is strongly stitched into our psyche because it originally served many vital purposes to maintain the survival of Our (prehistoric) Gang. Since biological functions changed slowly in the relatively brief period of time humanity has had a civilized existence, we have behavioral tendencies that essentially served well our caveman ancestors. Violence and hostility probably became genetically enhanced because they enabled leaders to maintain social order in the group and thus reduce conflict, protect against invaders, settle quarrels, discipline troublemakers, and decide on concerted action (Thorpe, 1974, p. 244; Bernstein and Gordon, 1974; Chauvin, 1977). There is one tragic change in the biological quality of aggression. Many species seem to have developed mutual signals in which the weaker combatant gives up in a conflict. These are called by ethologist Konrad Lorenz (1966) ritualized behavior patterns inhibiting aggression (p. 131) and by Remy Chauvin gestures of appeasement (1977, p. 226). Restraints against aggression occur because the apparent helplessness of a victim inhibits further attack (Bernstein and Gordon, 1974). Tragically, human beings have lost their primate-ancestral protection against murder and other aggression against a nonprovocative victim. Indeed, expression of pain tends to increase punishment when the aggressor is already angry, according to Rule and Nesdale (1976).

Aggression and sex come together. Our not very noble ancestors (dominant males) used aggression to keep straying females from fleeing (Bernstein and Gordon). This, of course, increased the likelihood of bullies passing along their genes to another generation of male chauvinists. However, some females were not above using their traditional wiles. There is evidence that females allied to high-ranking males use their status to enforce dominance against males that outweigh and potentially outfight them. Moreover, aggressiveness plays a role in sexual development in both sexes, says biologist J. Z. Young (1978). Those who take an idealized view of human relations will have to revise their view of the fair sex.

Anger probably accompanies sexuality, since the locale for its arousal in the brain is close to those centers which also integrate sex. Wilhelm Stekel (1929) went so far as to state that "there is no cruelty not toned with sexual pleasure. . . . Man is cruel for the sake of the pleasure which the barbarous act procures." The tendency for sex and anger to be simultaneously aroused causes them to be mutually reinforced, and consequently to be associated and expressed together.

PERSONAL ORIGINS OF ANGER

Anger is not learned. One has only to observe a frustrated infant to know that it arrived on this planet ready to do battle with its enemies as soon as it could identify (or misidentify) them. What is learned is the means of expressing anger and the (usually inappropriate) targets for anger. We are badly taught that it is appropriate to humiliate, punish, or destroy others. Or conversely, may be taught that even though we are in the process of being chewed up, it is morally wrong to defend ourselves. What you have probably not been taught is to make sure that you are demolishing the right person. Think of your training. Maybe you weren't even taught to ask yourself if you are a little bit to blame for starting the fight. Few of us are taught or subsequently learn the appropriate expression of anger in terms of defending our interests without making the situation worse.

Anger is aroused by *emotional pain, humiliation,* and the *belief that somebody is controlling us. Inferiority feelings* are accompanied by oversensitivity and vulnerability. We also cope with them by *humiliating others. Frustrated dependency needs* can be experienced as a direct aggressive attack. However, children do need some frustration to help them develop strength and independence. This helps to account for the sense of loss when a passionate opponent dies. Part of our identity is determined by who our enemies are.

Emotional deprivation. Illustrating the interrelatedness of all our feelings is the scientific finding of the connection between lack of closeness to one's parents or caretakers and a tendency to excessive anger. It has been discovered (Restak, 1979) that physical closeness, cuddling, and physically playing with infants enhance the development of their brain pleasure centers. Emotionally deprived people have problems experiencing pleasure. Individuals deprived of affection or closeness develop an extraordinary need for it which is unlikely to be fulfilled. This stirs them into violent reactions. Presumably this is true to a lesser degree for some problems with intimacy and experiencing pleasure.

Punishment. Curiously, punitiveness by mothers may even have an adaptive value (Bernstein and Gordon, 1974). It seems to create dependent offspring who seek their mother's protection when distressed, even if the mother is the source of the distress! Why? To keep baby from straying away where a nasty leopard might enjoy a tasty snack. You see, mothers are a truly discriminated against group.

Anxiety. This is a source of aggression. Theodor Reik asserted that hatred is experienced only for objects one fears. Some crimes are explainable as attempts to reduce anxiety. Innocent people are victimized because aggression reduces some people's tension or irrational fear of the other person or the group he represents.

IRRATIONAL TARGETS FOR ANGER

An irrational target is one that is either not the original source of our anger, or one to which the angry response is greatly excessive in terms of the provocation. Violence does beget violence, and the personal experience of being brutalized encourages seeking weaker targets of opportunity. Moreover, the model of violence, i.e., watching vicious attacks on others as in the movies or TV, encourages children immediately and subsequently to be violent or justify its use by others. Creators of popular media events demonstrating violent scenes are in my opinion criminals. Children are impressionable. They are likely to assume that what they have experienced or observed is the nature of the world. Thus they react with either intense anxiety toward subsequent threats, or they make plans to take vicious retribution. Sometimes the *child even identifies with the aggressive parents.* As Anna Freud conceptualized it: "By impersonating the aggressor, the child transforms himself from the person threatened into the person who makes the threat." Elsewhere we have discussed identification nuclei and fantasies of vengeance.

"Hostile identification with pain-inflicting parents" is another insidious form of irrational target selection in adult relationships (Parker, 1972a). I became aware in therapy groups that particular patients would often attack others for having certain traits. Since I knew the aggressor, after a while I saw a pattern in which he picked a target who had traits which he himself had. The despised trait which "justified" the attack was one which was possessed by a parent and experienced by the aggressor as very painful. Thus victim, aggressor, and pain-inflicting parent all had the same characteristic. The victim of the attack generally had not provoked the aggression. In this way, the sins of the parents are repeated by the children through unprovoked hostility to others.

Among the examples of identification with pain-inflicting parents I observed were the tendency to embarrass others, violence, passivity, critical attitude, sarcasm, and provocativeness. The reader might find it useful to consider what characteristics of his parents pained him the most, and to determine whether he not only has assumed these qualities but also is extremely critical of others who are just like him and dear old Dad or Mom.

AGGRESSION IN ADULT LIFE

Anger is probably the earliest feeling. It is maintained and expressed in extraordinarily complex and devious ways (Parker, 1972a). The ways we are provoked, and learn to handle anger, are far more important than sexuality in determining the particular qualities of our personality. Some of this we have already discussed in earlier chapters.

The social setting in which we find ourselves can increase or decrease the likelihood that strong anger will be expressed (Elliott, 1976). Moreover, once anger or emotional arousal exists (touchy, sensitive, inflamed moods) this increases the likelihood that somebody will do something to touch off the explosion (Rule and Nesdale, 1976). Whether this occurs is dependent upon whether the aroused person actually believes that his upset feelings are due to anger. If so, look out. Expression of aggression can affect brain functioning for perhaps twenty-four hours (Henley, Moisset, and Welch, 1973). Moreover, as a sado-masochistic primeval heritage, erotic arousal increases the effect of angry feelings on expressing oneself in an aggressive way (Rule and Nesdale, 1976).

What makes people angry? By reviewing this list you can become more sensitive to the feelings (and weak points) of others, and perhaps become aware that you yourself are overly sensitive or vulnerable. Individuals report anger for some of these reasons: frustration at being teased; not being liked; having one's arguments sidetracked; lack of respect; lack of honesty; having one's mind read (assumptions about what one is thinking); overgeneralizing; someone's lack of conformity to society; being stereotyped; not being seen as a human being; being told what one should do; inflexibility in a romantic argument; being insulted; being used as a sounding board but having one's answer disregarded; a critical, holier-than-thou attitude; not being permitted to express anger; helplessness; inadequacy; being deceived; frustrating real or unreal expectations of others; crowding; not having one's objectives understood; being ignored; somebody's reactions being unconventional; rejection; discourtesy; deception. A transit worker objected to little old ladies not paying their fare!

Because anger is so general, and sometimes so unpredictable, you have to guard yourself against the consequences of irrationality—in yourself as well as others! Moreover, you and your social or business contacts may be more vulnerable than you anticipate, so alertness to others' sensitivities is in order. Of course, the hypersensitive person is a problem to himself and others. Hypersensitivity is in my experience a problem for therapy, and one not easy to help.

Manipulation. Anger can be used as a manipulative "game" to obtain selfish ends. The aggressor is not angry but pretends to be so in order to obtain some devious goal. For example, one who is ashamed to *terminate a relationship* directly may pretend to have a temper tantrum in order to provoke the other party into taking responsibility for the breach. Anger may be used to *avoid confrontation* concerning the real nature of one's behavior. *Emotional blackmail* uses anger by creating fright in order to get what one wants. *Teasing* is a way of expressing hostility and humiliating a weaker target.

Anger serves many other significant social purposes (Novaco, 1976). By adding to our sense of being aroused, it *provides energy, yet it can disrupt our efficiency and interfere with communications.* Sometimes it causes *attention to be directed at important issues,* but it also *can keep people at a safe distance* as an evasive tactic. The person with the role of Angry Man (or Woman) uses fear to create and protect his *image of strength and dangerousness.* Being angry creates *a sense of personal control* or being in charge.

Emotional common sense suggests that you should own your anger, i.e., be aware when you are angry, and be able to use it in your best interest but without making a situation worse. The fruit of infantile use of anger is to be hated or treated with contempt. Should you be a constant victim, then your dignity requires that you not put up with a single further instance. Many bullies require being put in their place. They really are inviting punishment and laugh at you for not seeing through their games and their real need to be treated as the guilty people they experience themselves to be. Take no actions based on emotional blackmail. Let them be furious, threaten suicide, accuse you of being the cause of their death, and so on. Look them in the eye and inform them that since everyone has to die, you respect their strength to choose the time and place of their own death. If the offender will not cease, *get rid of him or her.* The odious skunk who avoids criticism through outbursts of anger ought to be told what a creep he is. Let him be angry. It's his privilege.

Censoring anger. It is manipulative to tell people when it is acceptable for them to be angry. The goal is "To be free to do what *I* want, but I want to get away with it because I will make you feel guilty or socially inadequate if you protest." Learn to recognize this strait jacket for your feelings: "How can you be angry with your mother?" "Crying is a copout." "It's OK for you to be angry, but don't show it here." During a political discussion while in a Jewish couple's home: "I'm tired of hearing about the Jews killed in Europe." Principal to supervisor: "You shouldn't be angry at that subordinate."

Provocation. The real motive is to dominate or justify separation, or to obtain punishment for guilt. It often happens in close relationships, and it is a pattern that ought to be stamped out by self-discipline in keeping one's mouth shut, refusing to start or continue the fight, psychotherapy, or firmly *ceasing the relationship* if nothing else helps. Some examples? A husband telling his wife about anything he does that makes him feel guilty. The mother who ceaselessly asks her daughter about all her activities, or is never acceptant in a calm way of bad news, mistakes, or new experiences. The employee who comes to work late repeatedly after being informed that this is intolerable to the higher-ups. Insistence on "having the last word."

Is it ever justified to express anger? The answer is that it is certainly justified, but you will have to face the consequences. While it is foolish to believe that you should always express your feelings, there are situations in which your well-being demands that you express your anger. I once asked a group of twenty-eight people if they had ever saved a relationship by not expressing their anger and not one said yes. Remember this if you hold back justifiable resentment for fear of being left alone. It doesn't work. Some people deceive themselves by believing that it is immature to become angry and show it. They believe that they must be rational, and they hold back their feelings to avoid being considered immature or unintelligent. While I was writing this, a woman I am counseling called to thank me for helping her to express her anger to her husband after more than two decades of marriage, even though she is seriously considering divorce. "Thank you for teaching me that it is better to express your anger, I never did it so directly," she said. However, I did have to counsel her that shrieking her resentment at her husband, and acting as though she knew all the answers, made a sensible response to her impossible.

The consequences of holding back anger. It is a serious, damaging condition not to be able to express anger. *First*, holding back anger involves the risk of such psychosomatic conditions as high blood pressure, muscular fatigue, and coronary heart disease (Friedman, 1980). Part of the treatment of patients with coronary disease is helping them to recognize hidden hostilities without explaining away the reasons for them or denying their presence. *Second*, holding back anger can result in an avoidance of the real issues between people. "Peace at any price" doesn't work. *Third*, holding back anger does not eliminate it. It accumulates and then becomes expressed unpredictably and in ways harmful to your best interests. To use a classic example, an employer bawls out a man, who in turn abuses his wife, who hits the kid, who pulls the kitty's tail. *Fourth*, holding back anger makes some issues larger than they really are, as when we ruminate about all of the injustices perpetrated on us, and then give some unfortunate a bill for twenty years of mistreatment. Do you want to be in the position of the man who feels, "If you tell somebody off after twenty years they will think you've gone off your rocker." Finally, to express anger is to give the other person some indication of your feelings, perhaps even that you care. Your lover or mate may feel that you are indifferent if "anything goes." He/she may be motivated to change the way he acts if he knows that it is upsetting.

Expressing anger usefully. It is important to understand what is making you angry. Therefore, try to determine whether the other person has a motive for degrading or harming you. Perhaps there is a misunderstanding, or it is possible that there is no intention to hurt. There may be some differences of standards which creates an illusion of provocativeness. No harm may be intended and you could be overly sensitive. Some discussion is probably in order to clarify the issues and take further action. As you proceed remain aware of the other person's feelings as well as your own. To be excessively accusatory can make the situation worse. There is a difference between "I am angry at the way you are treating me" and "You are no good." Unless you wish to terminate the relationship, don't automatically escalate your anger to that kind of exaggeration known as abuse. You ought to make it clear that you value the person but can't stand only part of him or her. By pointing out some of the hurtful behavior, you do not intend to "wipe out" your partner. It might be useful to indicate that you want to improve matters and are not interested in humiliating the other person. In most cases you don't hate the other person completely. Exaggeration or minimizing your feelings will certainly shape the course of the relationship. Do observe how the other person reacts when told he makes you angry.

I hate to say this, but it is barely possible that you have contributed *just a little* to the situation. It is true that you may be furious, but, my self-destructive friend, I know you. You are provocative. Don't deny it. Ask the other person what he is angry about. Also, find out if there is a repetitive element. Have you been provocative over a period of time? Have your communications been clear and free of teasing or of violation of the dignity of the other party?

Handling anger. What do people do when they are angry and they can't murder the target? Some chop wood, swim, jog, beat on pillows, go into the bathroom and scream, or open up the window and scream! Relaxation imagery (see Chapter 10) is great for substituting a more pleasant mood for rage when we are not in a position to do something about it.

I think that we might conclude this chapter with the following *emotional-common-sense criteria for appropriate expression of anger.*

1. *Select the right target.* Make sure the person you express

your anger at is the one who provoked you. Don't provoke a foreign war because you are angry with your wife.

2. *Relate to the issues that are making you angry*, not to the other party's genetic heritage or prehistoric events.

3. *Monitor the amount of anger*. Let the response fit the provocation. Divorce is not justified because hubby brought home the wrong brand of tuna fish.

4. *Express your feelings in a timely way*. It is better to express your anger early in a situation. Wait until the other party might be receptive. To add fuel to the fire is damaging. I often recommend that couples in conflict schedule some time in advance (when they might be relatively calm) to discuss problems rather than waiting until the next fight. They rarely do so, from which I conclude that fighting is great entertainment for them. Why not? Anger is built into the nervous system. Learn about it, control it, or with your defective brain it will destroy what you value.

12) Understanding and Overcoming Depression

Depression is certainly the most complicated of all the "darker emotions." It is the best example of how our lives are affected by complicated interactions between our bodily functions, our personal history, our attitudes, and important life events. There are so many pathways to depression that we can think of it as being a number of different conditions, having in common an unhappy attitude toward one's person and life, a sad mood, and pessimism about the future.

THE MEANING OF DEPRESSION

Depression is an unpleasant reaction that gives us a signal that something serious is wrong. Originally, in evolutionary times, this feeling guided our ancestors to get close to people when they were isolated by the loss of a mate. In this way, it is similar to anxiety. In modern life, the mechanism remains and can be activated easily. When we are depressed we should ask: *What are our feelings telling us?* The answer may be:

- "I want somebody to take care of me."
- "I want somebody to tell me that I am valuable."
- "Something is seriously wrong with my body."

BIOLOGICAL MECHANISMS

We have biological mechanisms that react when our attachment to people important to us is disrupted. Unfortunately, the same mood of distress can be aroused by loss of self-esteem, being fired, or receiving insults. Moreover, some people react to loss not by depression but by coronary heart disease, peptic ulcer, rheumatoid arthritis, and automobile accidents (Klerman, 1973). Chemical reactions in the bodies of parents grieving for their children differ from those of unafflicted parents (Hofer, cited by Tiger, 1979).

What seems to be an anxiety attack caused by fear of open spaces may be a sign of depression. Indeed, an anti-depressant drug (imipramine) is helpful in treating this kind of anxiety (agoraphobia) (*Science News 5/26/79.*) We have already seen (page 92.) that it is normal for children to be nervous when they are left alone. Thus depression is tied to anxiety, because it is a signal (originally) that we are abandoned. The feeling of being abandoned seems to be transformed by Your Defective Brain into depression.

Depression seems to involve a negative balance between the reward system of the brain (see Chapter 5) and a punishment system (Akiskal and McKinney, 1973). To experience an appropriate emotional life, particularly one in which we can enjoy ourselves and learn how to avoid stress and unrewarding situations, requires complicated chemical reactions in the brain. The circuitry and biochemistry is complicated. It can break down in a variety of ways. Various social and fantasy experiences affect it. Particular defects lead to an overly active and optimistic frame of mind, or a depressed, pessimistic slowing-down. More severe defects may cause extremes of high spirits (mania) or sadness (melancholy).

RECOGNIZING DEPRESSION

Depression essentially is a feeling of sadness. However, there are a variety of bodily reactions which may or may not accompany a depression, depending upon its origin. For example, a depressed person may be active (agitated) or lacking energy (retarded). Moreover, depression is often accompanied by such other moods as guilt, anger, sadness, loneliness, loss of interest, helplessness, hopelessness, inability to cope, and feelings of lack of self-worth. Here is how people I have known have described being depressed: "Weak; hurt; sleepy; slowed down; paralyzed; unable to do anything; disinterested in anything but my own problems; insurmountable problems; self-condemnatory; fear of the mood continuing; immobilizing, just difficult to give yourself a shave; everything coming apart and not being wanted; deserted; loss of my self-image; food doesn't taste as well; I wasted the day by sleeping twenty-two hours; I don't feel free to associate with people; disillusioned with life and unfulfilled."

What is generally common to depressed people is a pervasive sense of emotional pain that is present most of the time and colors all events that occur. The potential for depression to affect so much of our emotional life and bodily functions exists for this reason: The brain centers which are involved in pleasure/pain or reward/punishment are intimately connected with other parts of the brain (limbic lobe, visceral brain) that influence moods and feelings, motivation, sexual behavior, appetite, action, and the endocrine glands, as well as learning, thinking, and understanding the world.

DIFFERENT KINDS OF DEPRESSION

Endogenous (biological) depression. People sometimes become depressed without any apparent psychological disturbance. It is likely that a breakdown has occurred in the chemical reactions that bring signals from one part of the brain to another (neurotransmitters). The reward system may be understimulated or the punishment system might be working overtime. Chronic psychological problems that are not resolved after some reasonable period seem to cause the same kind of biochemical reactions that are the cause of endogenous depressions. An example might be a period of mourning that continues for so long that the person goes from a state of *grief* (normal) into one of *melancholy* (pathological).

How does one know if one has an endogenous depression? Some indications are: loss of interest in sex, food, or hobbies (D. F. Klein, undated); early morning awakening with inability to go back to sleep; weight loss; slow movements; insomnia, lack of energy; variations in depression at different times of day (generally worse in the morning) (Klerman et al., 1979; *Roche Report*, 4/1/79).

Medical conditions that can lead to depression: endocrine

disorders (particularly of the thyroid, adrenal, and sexual glands, which are very responsive to stress); alcoholism; hypoglycemia; vitamin deficiencies; anemia; disorders of the central nervous system like multiple sclerosis, or cerebro-vascular disease; post-partum (after pregnancy) psychosis; response to medications used for treatment of hypertension; and, some believe, using oral contraceptives. Even high consumption of caffeine (coffee, cola, over-the-counter and prescription medications) is suspected to be a cause of depression and anxiety in the condition called *caffeinism* (Greden et al., 1978).

It is essential that if you have an unexplained long-lasting depression, you consult a physician who is also knowledgeable about psychological reactions.

Since there appear to be a variety of endogenous depressions (Klerman, 1973; Maas, 1976), and the diagnosis of the different types is still insecure, selecting appropriate treatment may be slow. Endogenous depression is the kind of depression that is most likely to be aided by medication. My opinion about medication is this: I do not recommend it for depression where the cause is one of the familiar psychological ones (see below) and it has not been present very long. When depression has lasted a long time, one may speculate that there is either a basic medical problem, or continued stress has created a biological condition that may be aided by medication. In this case, a psychiatrist might have to experiment with a variety of drugs in order to select the right one. I strongly recommend that you do consult a psychiatrist if medication is in order and not any other medical practitioner. The indications for the use of these drugs, and their side effects, are so complicated that only a specialist is in a position to select the drug and monitor its effects. Moreover, you might test the alertness of your consultant by asking him about urine tests which suggest the possible cause of your depression. In this way, you may save yourself considerable time and avoid being experimented on.

Psychogenic depression. This occurs as a reaction to various forms of psychological distress. Examples are offered to demonstrate how psychological predisposition and the mishandling of various kinds of situations and emotions can result in depression.

• *Loss of a loved person.* The sadness we experience at the breakup of a relationship—such as death, divorce, or abandonment—causes loss of emotional support. However, the connection with anger is clear, because we may rage at the person: "Why did you leave me?" or "How can I go on living without you?"

A woman recalled: "I get holiday depressions. I was alone on Thanksgiving and was ashamed that my doorman saw me alone. I was in my room from Sunday to Sunday and didn't speak to anyone. I was mourning for my college-age children who are both alive but dead to me. I am angry, disappointed, and hurt that they don't want to bother with me."

• *Anger.* Since most of us are conditioned at an early age not to express anger, we are unable to deal appropriately with humiliating situations for fear of retaliation or further rejection. We hold back our anger, which can become *internalized*—directed upon ourselves. We abuse ourselves for being too cowardly to fight back. The original humiliation, abuse, or exploitation and our anger at ourselves for permitting it result in a *loss of self-esteem* and ultimately in depression.

A man commented about his supervisor: "I cannot talk to her about how she treats me because if I did we would end up enemies." (I asked him what he would like to say to her.) "You were really lousy to me. You didn't want to hurt me but you dominate people by praising them and yessing them to death. I have to *blame myself* for not speaking back to you. I'm not independent. I had the capability of handling a business situation by myself but not the self-confidence."

• *Shame.* If one has a strict conscience and has failed at some task, then self-reproach results from violating high standards. Obviously, this is one of the worst gifts that a parent can endow a child with: standards high enough to ensure certain failure.

As a woman put it: "My depressions were ignored when I was young, and I decided that I wasn't worth much. I was convinced that I made a total ass of myself. Finally I earned my own self-respect because I learned I had the guts to stick to overcoming some of the things that were wrong with me. Now I am allowed to make an ass of myself. I know it's only human. The twinge of shame passes quickly because I have overcome the conviction that I was worth nothing."

• *Exaggerated guilt.* Depression often results when people

have done something wrong by their standards, but experience their "crime" to be more serious than most people would. This is common among individuals who were raised in an atmosphere of criticism. Slight deviations from their standards of morality re-create their childhood experiences in which the pointed finger and abuse were common.

A woman commented: "I have a mother who's the original guilt-producing machine. She presses the button and makes me feel guilty, and then I am depressed. No matter what I do, it doesn't satisfy her. I happen to be a very good cook. When she comes, it's a disaster; she tells me about the cook she used to have. I'm scared of her." (At which point another woman said to her; "I told my mother she's a lousy cook. If after all these years you can't learn to cook a turkey it's pretty sad. No, the ground didn't open up!")

• *Damage to self-esteem.* If we are abused, reduction in self-respect frequently results in depression. The respect of one's peers is the adult's equivalent of acceptance and love by a child's parents.

"I'm depressed about my job. I have to deal with it to banish it from my life. Waking up knowing I have to go to work, or sitting at my desk, I'm overwhelmed by depression. As soon as I am in touch with my resources to get out of my job, the depression lifts. *I realize that I have options."*

• *Loneliness.* While loneliness differs from depression, it can contribute to it. I have seen quite a number of people in my practice, frequently single but also married, who complained about feeling depressed. They felt depressed but lacked many of the common symptoms of depression. Their basic problem was feeling alone.

"I can't be alone. I get very depressed. My self-image goes sharply down. When I reach a certain level, I can barely cook myself an egg or take a shower. I feel the desperation of loneliness or depression. I get out of it by not sitting still."

VULNERABILITY TO DEPRESSION

If you suffer from depression, or are concerned about someone who does, self-help or proper use of a psychotherapeutic or psychiatric consultant will be more likely to work if you can properly evaluate your situation or more rapidly provide useful information.

Women seem more vulnerable to depression. This is reported in all countries according to Weissman. The reasons are numerous:

• Sexual differences in monamine metabolism (relating to neurotransmitters) are consistent with our knowledge of factors which make depression in women more or less likely (Robinson et al., 1977).

• Women are trained to participate in fewer but more important relationships.

• Women are also encouraged to remain dependent and immature (the writer I quote is a woman, Maggie Scarf, so don't accuse me of being a chauvinist).

• Many women complain about unpleasant changes in their mood at particular points of their menstrual cycle, and they are sometimes helped by hormonal treatment for any irregularities (Klerman, 1973).

Genetic predisposition. There are many studies that indicate that moods and temperament can be inherited. The mechanism of any hereditary form of behavior is obscure. Frequently *the concurrence of both genetic predisposition and special life events is necessary to bring about the behavior.* Perhaps some *combination* of vulnerability to defects of neurotransmitters and also sensitivity to interpersonal conflicts or loss of reinforcement is needed. In this way, social events stimulate disturbed functioning of the reward center, and also the hypothalamus, which controls many supporting bodily activities (Akiskal and McKinney, 1973; De Montigny and Aghajanian, 1978; Leung, Glagov, and Mathews 1976). Genetic predisposition seems to make the absence of one's parents for an extended time or on several occasions more likely to result in an immediate or delayed depression.

Early separation from parents. I know one woman who as a child had a brief hospitalization. She was put in an oxygen tent and thus was not able to be with her parents, particularly her father. He was a distant person, and a visit from him at this time would have been particularly meaningful to her. She suffers from depression and other discomforts when she is even temporarily separated from her husband. When her father died, she took over the responsibility for his burial from her mother. She expressed so little grief that I put her under hypnosis to let her express her feelings. Then she wailed about wanting her father's love and her pain at watching him die—also while in an oxygen tent.

Negative thinking. Depressed people seem to take a very selective view of the world. They filter out good news and embrace disaster!

Low self-esteem. Self-devaluation causes one to see oneself as deficient in attractive qualities that are especially important, e.g., ability, looks, and intelligence.

Negative expectations. Pessimism leads to feelings of hopelessness and the belief that life will get worse.

Self-blame and self-criticism. If something goes wrong, it's your own fault, because of your own deficiencies (Beck, 1973).

Overestimation of rate of failure. The depressed person sees himself as less perfect than the facts warrant (Abramson and Sackheim, 1977).

Passivity. Depressed people tend to be unusually dependent, feel helpless, are more aware of their own reactions than of the outside world, tend to be unassertive, pessimistic, and see themselves as inadequate (Hirschfeld and Klerman, 1979). A prescription for avoiding rewards and goodies in life! One might even get depressed being near such a personality.

WHAT ABOUT SUICIDAL FEELINGS?

Here all the feelings of depression are magnified—expectation that the pain will go on forever, futility, hopelessness, withdrawal, guilt, self-reproach, and so forth. *It is positively inaccurate to believe that* "the person who talks about suicide will never commit it." Mention of suicide is a message to anyone who will listen. Do not stand idly by while someone you cherish and value kills himself or herself because *no one listened, so it had appeared that no one cared.* Suicide is accompanied by discouragement, disillusionment, and disappointment. It is motivated by the wish to destroy some hated part of one's personality, hostility toward someone who has become represented by an identification nucleus in one's fantasy life, desire for re-union with a dead loved person, or a need to expiate for guilt. A mid-life crisis often occurs around the fortieth year, when the need for fulfillment in love and vocation seems to be frequently disappointed. The safest course in case of serious suicidal feelings is psychotherapy or hospitalization. Certainly your attention should be directed *immediately* to the final chapter in this book on selecting a competent psychotherapist.

SOCIAL EFFECT OF DEPRESSION

The depressed person often feels guilt and reproaches himself. Consequently, others are motivated to help him, reassure him, make him feel better. However, whether as a victim of depression or as somebody closely associated with a depressed person, it is useful to be aware of *secondary gain,* i.e., special treatment given a troubled person. Should you be suffering from a long depression, then you ought to consider the possibility that you have extended its duration in the hope that others will be especially nice to you. Depression is a high price to pay for emotional support. On the other hand, should you be close to somebody suffering from depression, be aware that this could be a signal that you or others have not met the needs of the person, or are not letting him express feelings of anger or love. Depressed people sometimes have not learned to express need for support or resentment directly.

COPING WITH DEPRESSION

These ideas are a summary of workshop discussions I have taped, the professional literature, and my own clinical and personal experiences with depression. Indeed, more effort was required for this chapter on depression than for any other in this book. Since there are so many roads to depression, all of these ideas may not apply to you (or a depressed person you know), but do pick out those that relate to your situation (as you have come to understand it). I have included the personal expressions of people who have used particular principles to help them overcome their depression.

1. *Maintain good health.* Jogging is as good for depression as some kinds of psychotherapy (Griest, undated). I personally get

cranky when I miss too many days. People have said about exercise, "I feel great and when I speak to somebody they respond better to me. . . . Gets me away from myself and brings me up. I forget about a lot of things."

2. *Understand your depression.* Try to figure out why you are vulnerable, and how depression has come to be your way of showing stress. Do you accuse yourself unjustly? Are you slow in replacing lost loves? Are you too easily humiliated by loss of status and by cruel people?

• "I think and go over the experience. I try to penetrate why it happened. It is reassuring to feel I am what I am. I lost someone because I was just myself. I didn't do anything to cause him to reject me."

3. *Learn how to give yourself love.* Get into the habit of being kind to yourself rather than critical.

• "I do something I want to do with my life, something I enjoy." "I'm good to myself, go on a shopping spree, go among people."

4. *Activity is the opposite of depression.* If depression makes you slow down, remember that it is hard to feel depressed and be active all at the same time.

• "I go folk dancing or scrub floors." "I clean up, wash my hair, and then I feel ready to go. I get out. Any change works. Put one foot in front of another."

5. *Avoid loneliness.* Remember, sadness is designed to stimulate us to change a situation of feeling abandoned (Arieti, 1977). By searching for new ideas and new people, you will discover that the lost people and status becomes less indispensable.

• "I ask people who are alone to bring one dish to a meal." "I get into contact with people who care about me." "I put in ads for social contacts and was amused by the response." "I invite students or foreigners who are lonely."

6. *Build up your autonomy.* Develop the ability to feed yourself emotionally (Parker, *Living Single Successfully*). Don't tell yourself that the world is coming to an end if you are alone.

• "I use a hobby calling for total concentration, singing. Everything leaves my head, and when problems come back, they don't have the same importance." "Writing is all-consuming. It is wearing and rewarding, and takes my mind off things that worry me."

7. *Stage-manage successful experiences.* Overcome the habit

of "learned helplessness." This is the idea that no matter what you do, nothing works. Most people do not plan for successful events until it is too late. Then something dramatic and difficult is required to avoid disaster.

8. *Change your mood.* We can exercise influence over our darker moods by actively avoiding thinking of them. It is also good to recall pleasurable people and situations. Emotional pain can sometimes be relieved by concentrating on events and people that you admire and that have brought you pleasure.

• "I use humor." "A creative idea or an attractive woman makes me high." "I reject depression. I say to myself, 'Stupid, if *you* want to live like that, go ahead and do it. *I'm* not going to stand for it any more.' "

9. *Get your mind off yourself.* Depressive people are always aware of their emotional pain, and sometimes gain benefits through their suffering, i.e., reproach to life and people, or martyrdom and attention.

• "After the sudden death of my husband I fell apart, first I lost and then I gained a lot of weight. I would wake up, be frightened with rapid breathing and heart rate. As soon as I took my mind off myself I would lose my fright."

10. *Get rid of rage through self-assertion.* You may believe that nice people don't fight back. What would you lose if you replaced the hostile, destructive people in your life with warmer people more interested in your welfare? It is not dishonorable to be angry, but it is dishonorable to be a dependent coward!

• "This time I didn't cry. I got angry. It was rage and much healthier for me." What if you are not yet ready to attack a particular target, or the person is out of reach? Sock a punching bag or pillow until you develop a sweat. This is a physiological indicator of a change in your metabolism. Perhaps it will be a new phase of your moods.

11. *Stop negative thinking.* Depressed people frequently expect the worst and see themselves as inadequate and guilty. Perhaps you exaggerate obstacles and devalue your worth (Kovaks and Beck, 1978).

• "I'm working on risk-taking. Even if it's a terrible place, I go out and put myself on the line to meet new people." "After breaking up a twenty-six-year marriage, I slept, worked on my business. I felt organized, and used my time constructively."

12. *Develop your strength.* When I am bothered by something, I try to find out why, and then redouble my efforts to overcome this weakness.

• "You redevelop hope in other areas." "The more you cope, the easier it is." "I'm willing to tolerate the pain because I come out stronger and firmer." "When I was in a mess I realized I had control and was able to make changes."

13. *Improve your self-respect.* Perhaps what is common to all psychogenic depression is a loss of status, i.e., we feel less valuable than before.

• "I think that everybody should have a goal in life to do something for other people. If you have the desire to be of some service, you will feel your life is more worthy and you won't feel depressed."

14. *Improve your emotional support system.* This involves not only people but your own autonomy, or enjoyment of your own personality. Get substitutes. Reward yourself in ways that take the place of the person or events that used to be so pleasing. Take active steps to avoid being reminded of, or paying attention to, those old-time events that are no longer satisfying (Akiskal and McKinney, 1973). Particularly, end your relationship with destructive people, and replace them with those with whom you can exchange good feelings and emotional support.

15. *Enjoy your depression.* Even with grief and sadness, there might be some benefits.

• "I try to experience it as deeply as possible, and then I feel the loving feelings." "I look at depression as a form of rest. It's taxing to take action all the time."

If you don't think passivity is a form of rest, then turn to the next chapter.

13) Passivity and Lack of Self-Confidence

An appropriate subtitle for this chapter is "Not Being Real." To be unable to assert yourself is to subtract from your real self. To let others impose their will on you is to participate in a particularly obnoxious form of self-destructiveness.

IDENTITY AND PASSIVITY

Most people are not born passive. While some babies are very quiet and receptive, even these kids soon become trouble-making home wreckers if allowed to flourish! An example of how an independent, exploring mind is turned off comes from a talented woman I know, who through life says, "I haven't been able to please myself, only other people." Her mother played this revolting game with her:

> Turn to the east,
> Turn to the west,
> Turn to the one that you love best.

"Then my mother would turn me to her."

Our view of life is strongly influenced by the way in which we are treated as children. Some parental attitudes that contribute to a passive or nonself-confident identity include:

Overcontrol. "I know best what is good for you. I cannot guarantee your safety unless there is a very short apron string with no slack."

Humiliation. "I am much smarter than you. You are a really dumb kid."

Indifference. "I cannot take the time to teach you how the world goes around. You will pick up all the practical skills on your own."

Inability to give praise. "What, me encourage that snot nose to believe that he/she is competent?"

High standards. "If you are not Phi Beta Kappa by age fifteen, you are no child of mine!"

Whether one is self-assertive or compliant depends on one's view of the world and how one perceives his role in it (Piotrowski, Chapter 6, 1957). If you have been trained to consider your actions and feelings important, if the tasks assigned to you by your parents and teachers have been realistic, if you have been taught that some efforts may be followed by rewards, then you are likely to feel confident that you can influence others and meet your needs through your own actions. If, on the contrary, your wishes and feelings were disregarded, you were never permitted to win an argument at home, and you were encouraged to try to meet goals beyond your capacities, it is likely that you face life feeling that others are more competent than you. You are likely to feel inadequate and valueless and in moments of decision to react in a compliant or self-effacing way. The day before writing this chapter, I had a hypnotic session with a woman client of mine who had been raped the same week. She didn't tell me, but her father had called saying that she minimized the whole matter. Under hypnosis it evolved that while there had been two other people sleeping in the same apartment she didn't call for help. Her mother had beaten her several times for protesting about mistreatment. Even in a moment of desperation she had been deconditioned from feeling worthy enough to get aid.

If you act like the following people, you are certainly passive.

- React to others as though your needs are valueless and their will must prevail
- Pushed around by arrogant waiters
- Sleep with people you despise
- Let your immature children rule you
- Hate yourself for giving in to your inefficient or bullying supervisor
- Robbed by inefficient or thievish corporations.

Do you identify with the following complaints?

- Let others make decisions
- Lack ideas on how to spend your time
- Feel exploited
- Find yourself in situations you had sworn you would avoid
- Frequent the company of people whom you dislike
- Drink because others drink
- Eat to please your mother or hostess
- Have sex even though you don't feel like it
- Wear clothing or express ideas because they are "in."

True or False?

1. _____ I am passive.
2. _____ I am a coward.
3. _____ I am a chameleon in sheep's clothing.

HOW PEOPLE EXPERIENCE THEIR PASSIVITY

Lack of Self-Assertiveness

- "I was polite to everybody except myself."
- "Being patient and loving to everybody except myself was my cross to bear."
- "I couldn't even placate my cat [. . . boss . . . parents . . . children, you name it]."

Unwillingness to Have Calm, Forceful Confrontations

- "I have to say no too many times before people accept it."
- "I don't want to hurt people's feelings by saying you lied to me."
- "I knew my husband was lying about the fact that he was an alcoholic."
- "I've gotten used to his crap."

Giving Other People Control

- "My spirits go up and down according to what people do to me."
- "Intimacy is desperately important. I am lonely, helpless, and worthless if nobody wants me or my company."

- "I can't arrange good experiences by myself. Everything depends on me having a special man in my life."
- Here it is from the viewpoint of the all-powerful one: "No matter what he does or says, I don't believe it."

Lack of Identity as Independent

A woman who worked for a prominent publishing house was speaking about her attitude toward her job: "We're all slaves. We have no sense of independence. We are cowed by the structure. I don't remember that we are supposed to be our own agents." Then spontaneously she saw the solution. "Suppose I offer to another editor an article I write which was turned down by my present editor and my editor gets mad? That's his problem. You have to be a hustler type and push. You have to get your identity together so that you don't get daunted by the power structure."

GENERATING PASSIVITY

What are some of the signals people give themselves that cause them to lose their self-assertiveness? How do you pathetically reduce your ability to get what you want out of life? *Pathetic?* Yes. There are times when you are pathetic. Don't deny it. Just change. By the way, you will also have to exercise some self-discipline if you are to substitute rewards for the degradation you inflict on yourself through excessive compliance.

"*I don't know who I am.*" Should this be true of you, then you either let others' preferences and desires rule the day, or you assert yourself in an arbitrary way that doesn't meet your own needs. It might be so important to you to give the illusion of knowing your own mind that you appear to be stupid or capricious. Therefore, the first step toward intelligent self-assertion and decision making is having a clearer idea of your identity.

"*I don't know what I want.*" Think about the frustrations in your life (see Chapter 14). Now, try to connect your needs, your values, and your goals in some pattern of achievement. This approach will integrate your experiences and you will avoid inner conflicts and there will be some reasonable likelihood that you will reach a worthwhile lifestyle without excessive costs of money, time, and spirit. It is critical that you understand your particular needs and how you can reasonably fulfill them. Then you will be able to plan a lifestyle with which you are comfortable and which you find fulfilling. You should clarify your *goals*. These are conditions you wish to attain in the future. Thus, starting with your feelings of dissatisfaction, and a knowledge of what pleases you and is valuable, together with the turn-offs which are repugnant, you can plan your activities (and life) in such a way as to meet your needs and obtain pleasure according to your values.

"I am not competent." If you are dependent on other people in general, or on a particular individual, then you dare not antagonize them. To meet your childish belief that you must be taken care of, you sacrifice more mature needs, your ego, and a feeling of independence. It is not possible to conceal a wish to cling to somebody else. He or she surely knows your weaknesses, and either exploits you through control, resents your demands, or has contempt for your weakness. By being too weak to fetch for yourself, you lay yourself open to bullying, since you don't feel that you are in a position to antagonize your sole means of support. Fear of loneliness as well as feeling incompetent frequently keeps people in undesirable relationships (see Chapters 14 and 15).

A woman trained to feel incompetent. A middle-aged woman was very distraught because her older sister, upon whom she relied, was moving to another part of the country. "When I was young, my sister was told to help me with my homework. My mother wouldn't let me help around the house. I didn't feel competent when I grew up. I got my own way in everything, so my mother wouldn't have to scold me. Yet, my sister always criticized me. (She was the self-appointed mother after a while.) My mother was no mother while the other was boss. My sister now doesn't want to be my mother. (Fear of abandonment.) Then I expected her to be a sister, not a mother. I had a temper tantrum, and my sister slapped me in front of my mother."

"I am guilty or worthless." If you suffer from this malignant condition, you believe you are entitled to nothing. As a wrongdoer, a sinner, a violater of all that is sacred, you are lucky that the rest of us virtuous creatures even let you survive. Of course, should there be reasonable grounds for you to feel guilty, then it is self-destructive for you not to pay the penalty and try to

make amends. It is better to do this than let your life be blighted by feelings of sin. Unreal guilt feelings may require psychotherapy. However, some emotional common sense self-evaluation is indicated. I had a patient who went through life feeling guilty for the death of her mother when she was an infant. When she was to undergo surgery, she felt impelled to announce (no doubt to the astonishment of the surgical team) that she was being punished for her guilt in this tragedy. Our defective brain frequently accounts for our blaming ourselves for traumatic circumstances beyond our control. Then it retains this misinformation forever. Children frequently blame themselves for the death of parents or the break-up of marriages. They exaggerate their own power, feel guilty, and then retreat from expression of any personal power because of guilt.

"I expect to be a failure." There is evidence that people who expect to perform poorly actually do perform less well, choose not to engage in activities requiring genuine achievement, select less demanding tasks, and are more easily discouraged. Women in particular seem to have this problem, especially when the criteria of success are vague, or there are social or public standards by which they will be evaluated (Lenney, 1977). Fear of failure can rob you of self-assertion. How can you take a risk if you believe that you will fail? People with such beliefs experience themselves as washouts no matter what their objective success. Even with success and good decisions they do not enjoy the rewards, because they see their actions, productions, and their very person to be inadequate. One's standards may have been set too high by parents. Conversely, we may have been informed that we are and always will be failures. To prove that this isn't so, we will climb Mount Olympus. Well, by temperament or ability we may not be mountain climbers, and we doom ourselves to feelings of failure by not achieving that which is accessible (and even honorable). We have to recognize our own worth, and also to know when circumstances are stronger than we are. Somebody whose job is eliminated by a recession or the capriciousness of government grants is a genuine victim. Many millions of people have been unemployed in our time because of the stupidity and selfishness of powerful people. Failure is not sweet, but it need not be everlastingly bitter either.

Fear of failure can be associated with oversensitivity, a feeling of vulnerability, and low self-esteem. One who suffers from this will take no risks and assume no responsibilities. How does a vulnerable person meet new friends or better lovers? How can he say that this process or procedure will make his work more profitable, enjoyable, or efficient? How can he say he'd rather go to a symphonic concert than rock-and-roll (or the reverse)? Some worms can't assert themselves; and until they can, they will serve as bait on somebody else's hook.

"*My first obligation is to someone else.*" We have discussed the problem of unreal obligations, but it is worth adding here that *your first obligation is to yourself.* I remember being accepted as a candidate for training at a well-known psychoanalytic institute. When I tried to make out a schedule to accommodate my previous commitments and necessities, I was told, "Your first responsibility is to the _____ Center." My reaction (private) was that if my first responsibility wasn't to myself, then it was to the Veterans Administration, which was paying me a salary. These authoritarians were only offering me the opportunity to obtain about $2,100 worth of training in exchange for about $5,000 worth of my time at the rate they would bill their clients. I recall getting really tense, until I decided not to attend. When I called to state that I wasn't coming, I had a marvelous feeling of relief.

If you find that you are not asserting yourself, while others create burdensome demands upon you, try to determine whether they can do something for themselves. If they can, insist that they contribute to their own welfare. Tolerate their pain; it won't hurt you a bit. After all, you already have a good deal of emotional common sense! It may be reasonable to call upon third parties to assume their obligations. I have known people who took exclusive care of aged parents and let well-to-do or capable brothers and sisters get away with selfish behavior. If need be, express your feelings and get rid of selfish relatives. Above all, be careful in what you take from others in order to avoid new obligations. Learn how to work for yourself. Live your own life and meet your own needs.

"*I am afraid I will be out of a job.*" If you think that you and your family are inches away from welfare or the soup line, then you had better listen very carefully to that creep who hired you. After all, who are you to deprive your children of that expensive summer camp, your wife of that mink coat which makes her friends hate her, or those diamonds which she's scared to wear in public. Maybe that precious self-image of yours does require a Cadillac every year. You're going to a resort? Only the best accommodations will do. Well, stupid, the real cost of this is your economic fear and the necessity of making decisions on the basis of your employer's needs and not your own. *It is vital to develop a nest egg.* Then you can be yourself both on the job and off.

"I was taught to be polite and let others have their way." False ideologies also keep a person from defending his rights. One student told me of his inability to shut off a monopolizer in class. Since he was taught to be polite he could not risk losing his teacher's good opinion by expressing his feelings concerning the behavior of the other student. *It is often necessary to express your needs in a firm but non-abusive way.* Recently, when somebody left a radio blaring unattended on a beach, I went and reduced the volume. When the guy objected (he was quite some distance away) I told him that we were annoyed.

"I am not living in the present." Transference from other situations can ruin your self-assertion. A too-powerful father or mother, or religious or educational mentors, can create in you a tendency to be compliant with others who superficially share the same characteristics. Fear or incapacity to deal with particular classes of people—e.g., one or the other sex, authority figures, those with particular heights or qualities of voice—should alert you to the fact that you are transferring compliant reactions to the present from your childhood. You will be more self-assertive by living in the present and dealing with the so-called authority figure according to your present realities.

FROM PUTDOWN TO TOUCHDOWN

Here are a few successful suggestions to improve your self-assertion.

Develop Perspective

• See yourself clearly. Know your values and what you can offer to people.

• Learn the difference between opinions and facts. Most criticism is merely opinion.

• Rejection is painful, but it doesn't wipe you out as a person. Find a replacement.

• Do not compare yours with other people's strengths. As the great black baseball player Satchell Paige put it: "Don't look back, someone might be gaining on you."

• Don't assume that you can win them all. Winning even once in a while is great.

Eliminate the Negative

• Never allow yourself to be degraded.

• Many hurtful people actually resent you if you don't stop their sadism.

• Eliminate liars, phonies, and unreliables from your life.

• Don't lose in advance—go to bat and take your chances.

Learn How to Make Friends and Allies

• Recognize what you do that makes others uncomfortable.

• Reduce any attitudes of superiority. Accept others and do not impose your ideas and values.

• Learn social skills. There are sincere ways of gaining others' cooperation, respect, and affection.

• Be trustworthy. This is the road to getting others to work in your interest.

• Accept warmth. It will do wonders for you and those around you.

• Learn to offer warmth. It too will do wonders for you and others.

Work on Your Motivation

Take this pledge for action: You will take the time to repeat out loud and in front of a mirror these self-signals listed below as many times as is necessary to improve your morale. As you do this conscientiously, your feelings about yourself will improve. Further, you will spontaneously change these messages in such a way that you will be able to realize more clearly those particular problems or ways of seeing yourself that cause you to be self-degrading. Be creative in psyching yourself up!

• I will learn to like myself.

• I must stop pleading.

- I must be strong.
- I will not let others push me around.
- I will be self-reliant.
- I will _____ (you name it).

You can have strength and self-direction without the cost of anger, hostility, sulking, or self-degradation. You can change so that you will neither be pushed around nor need to exploit others. You can experience some personal authority.

Remember to become more self-assertive. Self-respect will be yours if you reduce compliance to others and express your needs and wishes in a definite way.

14) Overcoming Loneliness and Deprivation

The twin pains of emotional deprivation and loneliness are a great burden, and self-destructiveness frequently prevents people from overcoming them. They afflict even those with large and active families. How many people who kill themselves leave behind parents, spouse, children, and friends? If you have difficulty feeling close, even in a familiar milieu, I can imagine your fears of strange locales or crowds where you may be shy or unknown!

There are different ways of feeling estranged. *Deprivation* is the feeling of lack of love which stays with us when a parent or other loved person is dead, rejecting, or disinterested during our period of growing up. *Loneliness* can occur at any age. It is characterized by the feeling that there has been no closeness for a long time. *Alienation* (Beck and Young, 1978) is the belief that one is completely different from other people. *Exclusion* means that one feels that one is not part of a group to which one would like to belong.

The need for contact is built into your nervous system (Chapter 3). Perhaps contact is the stimulus for your very feeling of being alive and human. As young children, we learn our self-image in part through seeing others. We also sense our bodies through being tossed into the air by our parents as well as being touched, fed, cleaned, warned, hurt, threatened, and so on. Both physical contact and emotional responsiveness add to the feeling of being loved. To the child, not to be caressed is equivalent to being told that he is unlovable. I have had many homosexual male patients who reported that they were never kissed or held by their fathers. Other people have expressed different problems of relating if a parent died at an early age, or when one parent was physically present but seemingly indifferent to the child. One man said that he was angry at his father for not taking an interest; he didn't know if his father loved him or hated him.

Individuals who feel emotionally deprived later on have special problems. Often they do not feel self-assertive enough to make friends easily or meet suitable mates. They are the people who are so emotionally hungry that ordinary expressions of love, affection, and sex leave them unfulfilled. *Nothing is good enough.* Ask yourself whether people have complained that you are never satisfied, demand too much, or are just plain hard to please.

One of the oddest aspects of emotional deprivation is that many people who suffer from it do not know it! We pay such a price as children for being dependent that as adults we will not admit it to ourselves. Some people see themselves as totally incompetent, so that in desperation they clutch onto others. If one clutchee cuts off from the emotional octopuslike tentacles and flees, the clutcher will soon find another victim.

Thus there are twin dangers in feeling emotionally deprived. Isolation and loneliness are particularly unpleasant feelings for such a person. If the deprived person yields to his feelings, which are unreasonable from the point of view of those around him, then sensible people become defensive or flee, seeing him as inadequate, dependent, and insecure. If he denies his needs, then he does not find people who are emotionally expressive and can nurture him. If at any time there is no one catering to the hungry one, he experiences a feeling that is dreaded: *loneliness.*

One of the most revealing aspects of discussing emotional problems with literally thousands of people in open participation/discussion groups that I lead was the central theme of loneliness in their lives. In the midst of New York City, which, if you hadn't heard, is pretty crowded, these people were lonely or feared loneliness. Emotional starvation in the midst of plenty. Fear of starvation in an ice cream parlor.

Many people make profound decisions because of fear of loneliness, just as many others do for fear of anxiety. Loneliness is their most dreaded feeling. Mates, children, friends, and neighbors are all tolerated, when the plain facts are that these individuals are tearing away at their emotional flesh. These people dare not move away. They are afraid to defend themselves against sadistic husbands and wives, or they maintain noxious "love" relationships because they dare not lose their tormentor. Love, indeed. Cold, cringing, nauseating fear of being alone. A total lack of confidence that a more loving or accepting friend or mate can be found.

Fear of rejection is also characteristic of lonely, emotionally deprived people. The relatedness, the contact which will warm their spirits, is hampered by an oversensitivity and lack of self-confidence. Do you believe that if you don't get too close you can't be rejected? Can you approach a stranger at a meeting who seems to have a compatible point of view? If unmarried, can you smile at a stranger across a crowded room? If a newcomer whom you might like wants to make contact, can you lend a helping hand? No? Then you are self-destructive and need all the help you can get.

Among the self-destructive ways of avoiding rejection and loneliness are having sex with total strangers in order to have a companion, always mixing with a crowd so that the feared intimacy is not risked, or "running around town to oases to get emotional support." You may also deceive yourself into believing that a cold, poor relationship is valuable.

Fear of commitment is also frequently experienced by lonely, emotionally deprived people. They do not see themselves as strong enough to protect themselves from the stresses of relationships. Perhaps they feel that they are so cold that the other person's reasonable needs for warmth will completely deplete them. Frequently the turmoil of their households which led to their own deprivation caused them to fear entering into a relationship which would repeat the pain. Thus the very warmth which would relieve their misery represents a tender trap of commitment and causes them to become anxious and run away or spoil a good experience.

Alienation is a closely related problem. To feel different from other people, to be unable to relate to events and institutions meaningfully, to feel emotionally distant from everything and everyone, is a guarantee of loneliness, deprivation, and feelings of rejection. A member of an oppressed minority forced to re-side among those who have contempt and hatred for him maintains a better adjustment by feeling distant from his tormentors. However, some people feel alienated as a neurotic defense against feelings of insufficiency. Here it takes the form of superiority feelings. After all, "only pagans, apes, or barbarians could treat me the way they did." Such attitudes are frequently developed by bullied or scorned children. They isolate them even after they have the strength and mobility to surround themselves with friendly faces. Other people become alienated because of narrow-minded parents and teachers who did not educate them to the differences between cultures, to the valid customs of other groups, to techniques of understanding newcomers in order to communicate with them as equals on the basis of shared humanity. To such unfortunates, all the people of the world except for the few with whom they group are permanently outsiders.

What are the symptoms of alienation? To be alienated is to be unable to enjoy meeting new people; to operate on the periphery of events; to see life as "sliding through a nightmare, with nothing real"; to feel "boxed in and turned off"; "having to have a plastic personality in order to survive"; to lack common interest with others. Do these symptoms fit you? Don't give up. They're curable.

Making and keeping friends is an important solution of the problem of loneliness, deprivation, and alienation. This may come as a surprise to those of you who feel that a love relationship is what you really need, preferably an unrealistic, idealized, romantic, epic musical with a cast of thousands directed by Cecil B. De Mille. Forget it. These are merely adolescent fantasies you developed when that little girl went to the junior prom with the gorilla from the other class, or when those pimples on your face convinced you that you would go through life unloved.

Making and keeping friends is a psychologically important factor in its own right. It creates an atmosphere in which we can avoid the worst effects of stress and its emotional discomforts and can also create a pleasant frame of mind in which we can face other problems. Friendship will by itself help to overcome tendencies to deprivation, loneliness, and alienation. While friends are not a complete substitute for a loving physical relationship, they create some feelings of satisfaction which can tide one over until such a closeness is achieved.

I asked a large group of people what characteristics they required in their friends. Check their answers so that you can compare them with your own requirements and see also whether you can meet the needs of others: non-competitiveness; sensitivity; reliability; acceptance; initiative; commitment; support; kindness; generosity; sincerity; not pretending the other person is something he's not; being understanding in the face of depression; having common interests; rapport or tolerance for each other's crazy ways; honesty; communication on a real level; getting something from one person not possible from someone else.

There are several key issues in making and keeping friends: taking the initiative to form the relationship; achieving the optimal degree of closeness; giving and taking; honesty and criticism; trust; and shared activities.

It should be obvious that no friendship can be started without one or both individuals taking the initiative and in some manner expressing interest. This is obviously a matter both of good judgment (that the other party is interested) and taking a risk. Very likely some approaches are not welcomed, either because of the ineptitude of the initiator or because he or she is perceived as having too radically different values or lifestyle from the other party. The possible nature of rejection should be considered and added to one's stock of worldly wisdom to avoid making similar mistakes in the future. This, however, is not an invitation to cowardice. Repeat: If you remain as cowardly as you have probably been in the past, you will be stuck with deprivation.

The ultimate degree of closeness which is desired and the speed with which it is approached are two of the most important considerations in forming a friendship. It is a matter of frequent observations that strangers traveling together exchange the most intimate revelations and then split, signifying that the maximum of intimacy is no proof of friendship and may signify nothing. I have known individuals with whom I would have liked to have friendly contact flee from me after too deep a personal revelation on their part. They experienced shame, although I myself did not look at them critically. Therefore, it is important to be aware of the other person's reactions. Be sensitive to possible discomfort at your expression of feelings and experiences or to a front you put up which keeps you from being known.

Giving and taking are important parts of friendship. I know of one relationship (you can decide for yourself whether it was a friendship) where two men played chess on a weekly basis for twenty years. At the end of that time they ceased the game and never saw each other again. They entertained each other without commitment, then called it quits.

The subject of givers and takers is important enough to be discussed. Let us consider the psychology of being a "giver." To some individuals, this is a vital role, and they feel very uncomfortable if they cannot assume it. They are probably covering up deep feelings of inadequacy. They (you) can be recognized by being excessive tippers, never letting the other person pick up the bill, throwing overly lavish parties, selecting as companions deprived people, and so forth. What are the effects of this compulsive kind of behavior? The person who said, "If you care for somebody, it's not draining," is probably in the minority. More frequent are such comments as "Always the crying shoulder"; "It's good to be giving, but after five years it's too much"; "What am I getting out of it"; "You put yourself in an inferior position by always being a sounding board"; "I'm tired of being told how good I am by people who benefited and then went to someone else."

Individuals who see themselves as independent, perhaps even as givers, can experience deep frustration in their emotional needs. They pride themselves on their self-reliance and emotional generosity. Woe to them in a prolonged crisis. They are like the car that cannot get started on a wintry day because the battery is drained and the oil congealed. I know one woman who sprained her ankle on the street and was afraid to ask for help because she experienced as repellent the image of helpless old people.

Let us consider the reactions of people to "takers": "Making her feel good made a wreck out of me, so I split"; "The most famous giver's reward was in heaven"; "A taker in giver's clothing"; "Takers are selfish and insensitive." If you are a taker, beware. You will be seen through and rejected, and then have to clutch on to someone else. Have a heart! Should you be a giver, learn to recognize the takers. They are sometimes the underprivileged of life. Sometimes they are people who are trained to exploit others through having been spoiled or by the training and example of selfish parents. Frequently they are individuals who are going through a traumatic, stressful period because of some separation or loss of a loved person on whom they are dependent, and anybody is game to be shot down to meet their needs. *There is a difference between having compassion and being a sucker.*

What, then, is an approach to giving and taking which shows emotional common sense? *First,* you have to be prepared to ask for and willing to accept warmth in order to enjoy it. *Second,* material and emotional gifts are not completely interchangeable. Be aware of this both as offerer and recipient. *Third,* to give gifts is no guarantee of stability. That is, be aware of all facets of the relationship and of events in the other person's life. Do not accept gifts of great value, knowing you feel like separating, unless you are a rotter or enjoy big sordid scenes. *Fourth,* expressing concern is not the same as remedying a situation. Whether you or your friend is in the position of giver or taker, realistic considerations may require assistance, not just expression of feelings. *Fifth,* be appreciative. If you cannot say "thank you" genuinely, discipline yourself to do so. *Sixth,* learn the difference between realistic and unrealistic obligations. To expect someone to be obligated to you when he does not feel obligated is to make demands and be disillusioned by the breakup of the friendship. Neither feel obliged to meet others' expectations of you nor demand that others meet your expectations. Let everyone live his own life, but be alert to expressions of emotional generosity freely offered.

Honesty and constructive criticism are certainly part of friendship, yet they destroy more friendships by mishandling than any other experience. The chief problem is that many people cannot recognize the difference between honest helpfulness on the one hand and degrading put-downs on the other. Even a helpful comment or a mildly worded criticism can be misinterpreted by an overly sensitive person to be a malicious attempt to hurt. On the other hand, the feeling of superiority, the intention of maintaining the other person in an inferior position, can be in the guise of an attempt to help. What is probably needed is a sense of timing. The person who is in trouble wants emotional support and not criticism. Oh, you insist on telling the truth at all times? Well, clod, no wonder you have no friends. When the crisis is over, then there is time to approach your friend in a gentle, querying manner, perhaps offering an impression, suggesting that he didn't foresee the consequences of certain actions—certainly not implying stupidity or basic inferiority which couldn't be helped. Sympathy and regrets are always in order, even if the results could have been foretold in advance. If you feel that you have gently and honestly tried to help the other person overcome some weakness or fault and the result is that you are snapped at, you must explore whether you have really been offensive or your friend "just can't take it." Then act according to your own needs.

What about receiving criticism? Frankly, I hate being criticized. However, I have disciplined myself to listen to it, at least momentarily. To reject criticism is probably to lose valuable information which can help you overcome self-destructive behavior. However, when a person is constantly critical, then one risks having one's good spirits and morale ruined, and it is wise to separate yourself firmly from the abrasive personality who values his hostility more than your good will. Also, you must become aware that if you are excessively sensitive, it is an example of your defective brain misleading you. After all, what you are still doing is feeling the hostility of parents and other people in your early life instead of relating to the current world as it is.

Two of the most beautiful feelings in friendship are trust and reliability. Friend will offer friend the confidence that his interests will be respected. This may mean not breaking confidence, not abusing or criticizing the other person in public, certainly not taking away one's money, mate, or job. I personally value reliability most highly. It is my philosophy not to deal with unreliable individuals no matter what their other values. If someone does not fulfill a promise or other genuine obligation, makes a habit of breaking appointments (particularly without letting me know in advance), does not return money, he does not get a further chance. Let others support his delinquency. My life is too valuable to me.

OVERCOMING BARRIERS TO INTIMACY

1. *Live in the present.* Preoccupation with past neglect and mistreatment makes your mood worse. You risk becoming unattractive. This is particularly true when one displaces anger from past situations to current ones. It even contributes to "nice" loving sado-masochistic relationships.

2. *Don't expect people to compensate for previous deprivations.* You will become a clutcher or a malcontent driving away potentially warm and supportive friends.

3. *Learn how to accept warmth.* So many people will respond well to being experienced as giving, valuable individuals.

4. *Learn how to offer warmth.* Closeness and an exchange of personal experiences are more likely with an affirmative, caring person.

5. *Build an atmosphere of trust.* Remember, people put up a wall around themselves because their feelings have been violated before. Misusing confidences and expressions of intimate feelings puts others on their guard.

6. *Good will.* An active interest in your partner's or friend's welfare creates a pleasant atmosphere, leading toward intimacy.

7. *Be reliable.* Do what you say you will do. The fastest way out of my life is not to fulfill a promise or genuine obligation. When somebody is casual about breaking appointments or doesn't return money, it is an unannounced trip to Nowheresville.

8. *Learn to be tactful.* Be sensitive as to which topics can be discussed, and recognize the right time and mood to bring them out. (Don't let oversensitivity keep you from confronting issues important to your own integrity.) Respect others' privacy when appropriate.

9. *Recognize others' and express your own signs of acceptance.* Well-meant compliments, enthusiasm, interest, and requests for more information, can make you more attractive and encourage the lowering of barriers between you and somebody you value.

10. *Recognize the limits of any relationship.* Have a variety of

friends, meeting different needs with various others, rather than demanding complete fulfillment with one person: chess with one, sex with a second, opera with a third, bowling with a fourth.

11. *Take a few risks.* Try to be friendly with new people. You may find that an occasional rejection is less painful than being alone or remaining with unfulfilling individuals.

12. *Learn to understand people.* When you find out their motives, you will discover whether or not they share your need for closeness and can be trusted with your intimate feelings.

13. *Be valuable.* If you want people to seek you out, and also want to experience enhanced self-esteem, do something positive for others.

15) Substituting Constructive for Destructive Relationships

QUESTION: What is the world's biggest violation of emotional common sense?
ANSWER: Remaining in a terrible relationship.
QUESTION: What is the greatest work of fiction of the human brain?
ANSWER: The weak-minded rationalizations people offer for staying while their partner uses them for a target.

There is something about human nature that causes far too many of us to put up with bad treatment. This conspicuous defect of human nature makes mincemeat out of such simplistic principles of behavior as "the pleasure principle" (people seek rewards and avoid punishment), the "reality principle" (we understand what is really going on, and thus can take successful actions), idol worship of the human brain ("How truly marvelous it is to have all those lovely billions of neurons all neatly hooked up to each other"), and so forth.

My clinical practice and contact with thousands of individuals in workshops and lectures suggests that destructive relationships cause more grief than any other emotional problem. The most fanciful idea since the invention of Santa Claus is the fantasy that decent treatment will prevail over nastiness or indifference. What about you? Is there now, or has there been, a destructive situation chewing at your guts? If you have put up with some sordid business or chronic dissatisfaction needlessly, you are reading the right book! To illustrate: As I wrote this chapter, a woman friend of mine called me and related that after many years, she had dropped a man she was associating with. "I wish I had had the strength to do this years ago." She was dissatisfied and knew that this relationship was wrong for her. She had let lots of good living go down the drain.

RECOGNIZING DESTRUCTIVE RELATIONSHIPS

You may ask, Why write about the obvious? Because (1) some people do not understand the origins of their emotional distress, and (2) some acquire the courage to make decisive changes when they recognize in others destructive experiences, attitudes, and habits like their own.

Let's bring to stage center the nature of destructive relationships and afterward some reasons that defective brains offer to hang around while their owner's life is wasted.

• *Sado-masochism.* Using one's spouse as a target for old angers. "Dear, who will play victim tonight?"

• *Loss of peace of mind.* Experience of anger, fear, frustration, low self-esteem. "Peace could be really wonderful, if only I really wanted it."

• *No communication.* Serious issues are avoided and your feelings are not taken seriously. "My ideas really aren't important, anyway."

• *Bad treatment.* Bad treatment is accepted. "I am comfortable with abuse."

• *Unreasonable demands.* One-sided relationship feeding your partner's infantile needs. "Anything you want, dear."

• *Inhibited feelings.* Anger, sex, and dependency are not responded to. "In my family we didn't bother our parents."

• *Discrepant lifestyles.* The preferred pattern of spending energy, time, and money is different. "We used to kiss all night, what happened to us?"

• *Lack of growth.* The normal flowering of ideas, abilities, and interests is hampered. "Nothing must change since those romantic days of our courtship."

Personality problems. There are a number of psychological factors which make people tolerant of destructive relationships.

1. *Low self-esteem.* Bad treatment and poor conditions are experienced as acceptable (see Chapter 1).

2. *Lack of autonomy.* The belief that one cannot function alone.

3. *False values.* One must sacrifice to one's family and children. Also, to leave is an admission of failure.

4. *Transference.* The marriage or other relationship is an attempt to complete unfinished family business from an early age.

5. *Lack of self-confidence.* The belief that one cannot solve life's problems by oneself.

6. *Lack of identity.* One's only role in life is as a wife, husband, or parent.

You can see that all of the emotional problems that contribute to self-destructiveness can keep you in poor relationships.

Why do people stay? Let's have a close look at the weaknesses that rationalizations attempt to conceal.

- *Laziness.* "It's a big effort to start over."
- *Preference for the familiar.* "It's hard to break a habit."
- *Fear of being alone.* "It's better to sit in the movies with someone."
- *Feeling unlovable.* "I don't know when that vacuum will be filled again."
- *Need for approval.* "I don't want it said I am copping out."
- *Cowardice.* "I am unwilling to confront and then face the pain."
- *Phlegmatic disposition.* "More time and energy needed for breaking it off than it was worth."
- *Neurotic guilt.* "The Inquisition won't like it. I would be doing something terrible."
- *Indecisiveness.* "There is always something good to build upon and something bad that can explode."

Gaining the strength to leave. I recently asked a group of single people how they gained the motivation to leave destructive relationships. Some of their comments:

- "I realized that there was nothing at home for me."
- "After five years of marriage, I exhausted all my efforts to change the relationship. My psychotherapist helped me."
- "Your books gave me strength."

• "Finally I realized that I could dump the relatives in my life. Years ago I would say, 'Oh, no, that isn't the right thing to do.'"

BETTER LOVE RELATIONSHIPS

Lest I be accused of being the Pied Piper of Singledom, i.e., leading people away from those nice loving, fulfilling, comfortable, romantic, growth-enhancing relationships they are now enjoying, into the boondocks of The Singles' Scene, let me say that being alone is not a fate worse than death, but living with somebody you don't care for can be. Here are some of the qualities which are often ignored by people who stay in destructive relationships.

- *A sense of security*—feeling safe
- *Warm feelings*—active exchange of affection
- *Good will*—protection of each other's best interests
- *Permission to develop*—personal growth is enjoyed and is not a threat
- *Balance between autonomy and closeness*—offering warmth yet respecting any need to be alone
- *Reliability*—support in time of distress or trouble.

WHAT IS A GOOD LOVER?

There are some people who would have the courage to answer this everlasting question, but I lack the requisite degree of presumption. My wariness is based on my belief that people's needs differ considerably—and on the evidence of my own eyes. People pair off in ways that surprise even the psychologist. Marriages survive that amaze friends who know the couple intimately.

It is useful to consider some of the following list of characteristics expressed by a group of adults. It will alert you to your own strengths and deficiencies and perhaps make you aware of some qualities important in good love relationships which you have underestimated. Try to measure yourself and a lover against this expression of group feelings concerning what makes another person attractive:

"Physical appearance; voice; personality; warmth; mutual understanding; sexual gratification; enrichment; acceptance; lack of exploitation; ability to listen makes one relaxed; ability to make one feel very much alive; lack of nagging; tenderness and expression of love; romance and sex; genuinely interested and noncompetitive; compatible and communicative; has qualities I want in myself; cheers me up; intellectuality; strengths; gives and receives warmth from the pleasure that I can give; confidence in self; realizes own positive traits; would feel it was worthwhile to have known me."

My personal reaction to this list is mixed. While it is pleasantly free of materialistic and unreal expectations, it also ignores considerations of lifestyle which enhance satisfaction or could provide important irritations.

Again, how did a group of people respond to the question *"What enhances your capacity to express love?"* Since inability to express love is a common problem, you might consider some of these ways to helping your mate be more expressive. This way you will create the circumstances in which your own capacity to express love is increased.

"When the person is unusually perceptive; when he does not see me as a stereotype; when I feel better about myself; when I can be of use; when I can fulfill a need of his; when the other person has a lot of feeling for me; when the other person doesn't disapprove of an open display of feelings; when I am relaxed; when there is a sense of trust; when he needs me and I need him; when he wants me and I want him; when there is a feeling of being accepted and comforted; when he treats me with gentleness and proper respect as a human being; when he knows me and doesn't expect something else; when he wants to do something for the other person; when the person understands my priorities."

A similar review of your relationship might follow this expression concerning the question *"What hinders your ability to express love?"* Remember, even nature needs a little help:

"Difficulty in asking for anything—I couldn't even ask for a hot dog, because I'd feel like a pig; wanting the other person to make the first move; premature commitment is an encroachment on me; receiving more than giving; a crazy need for control and to push me around; fear of being rejected; asking for more than I am willing to give; not feeling I deserve affection from this person; fear of responsibility."

You might now review some ways of increasing your own ability to be expressive.

Before we approach directly the question "What is a good lover?" I would like to make a comment about women's experience of orgasm. Until quite recently, most professional persons in the area of human relationships would have stated that a woman's inability to have orgasm is prima facie evidence of serious sexual maladjustment. Orgasm for both sexes is a complex psychological-endocrinological-neural-muscular-vascular response. I suspect that it is more complex in the human female than the male; and perhaps relatively minor circumstances can prevent a woman from achieving orgasm. *It is useful to distinguish between the experience of orgasm* (or its absence) *and the reaction of either partner to that experience.* In the days when it was assumed by some individuals that women were not interested in sexual experience, lack of orgasm was not noteworthy. Today, some concern is warranted, but caution must be exercised not to magnify the problem.

It is difficult to achieve a proper perspective in one's sexual life. People who have sex minimize it; those who don't have it exaggerate its importance! There are cases where a couple are happy in many respects but one or both partners are sexually dissatisfied. What sometimes occurs is that one partner assumes either that the other is sexually incompetent or disturbed or that he himself (or herself) is the culprit. Blame is experienced or attributed, and the degree of tension in the relationship increases substantially. In these circumstances, satisfaction and the capacity to please one's partner become hampered. The importance of lack of orgasm is exaggerated, and tension and dissatisfaction affect the emotional tone of the rest of the relationship.

What are the facts? Many women do not have orgasm with regularity. Of these, a large proportion state that they are sexually satisfied. It seems likely that their experience could be improved. However, it is the height of presumption to insist that they are not satisfied. If a couple experience sexual gratification when the woman is not achieving a climax, then one must be certain that the cure is not worse than the condition.

What then, does emotional common sense suggest? Awareness of this problem might serve as an occasion to review the relationship. I suspect that this is rarely done except in a crisis, with arguments and recriminations. I believe that the couple should express their feelings about the condition and whether either of them feels that it is seriously hampering their sexual enjoyment. If this should be the case, then it would be useful to get both a medical and a psychotherapeutic consultation. Often a gynecologist or other physician cannot serve as a consultant in the psychological aspects of the sexual experience. However, there are sometimes remediable conditions which prevent a woman from achieving orgasm, and these should be ruled out. It might be useful for the medical consultant to provide education for the man or for both partners. I know of one case where after years of marriage a husband could not locate his wife's clitoris. He was very rejecting of her sexuality because she refused variety. She, in turn, had refused to consult a gynecologist for years to see whether there was any medical condition interfering with her responsiveness. Both partners had attitudes which prevented them from enjoying sex, and the bedroom became a battlefield.

Being a good lover requires enthusiasm; it implies pleasing the partner. But it also requires a receptive attitude. It means that you expect and are willing to experience pleasure. Consider the complaint of one man that "a two-hour orgasm is a chore." There are lots of things that people can do if the orgasm comes more expeditiously. They can play Mozart duets on the piano, they can read poetry to each other, perhaps they can even go so far as to talk to each other. But holding back one's climax too long in order to control and gain the utmost from one's partner leads to self-destruction.

What, then, is a good lover? I think that a good lover is first of all knowledgeable and open-minded. Some reasonable balance is required between technique and the spiritual qualities of the relationship. There are plenty of sexual manuals available which can give you guides to variety and other ways of enhancing sexuality.

I think that a positive attitude toward sex and one's partner during the experience is also essential. To bring into the bedroom one's needs to be dependent, to express hostility, to dominate, to reject, and so forth is an invitation to frustration. These unresolved problems lead to such disorders as premature ejaculation or potency problems in the man and frigidity or refusal to have sex in the woman. Leave your problems outside the bedroom or you will have to resort to the advice offered by one person: "Mark it on the calendar." Many couples start fights outside of bed or in bed, but don't realize that they can resolve some fights in bed. If they could attempt to enjoy sex detached from their other conflicts, the bond between them would be strengthened. I have had clients who refused to take the sexual initiative or whose mates refused sex for long periods. In these cases, with the total breakdown of positive sexual feelings, the task of improving their relationship seemed hopeless.

What about the question of *commitment?* This can't be answered without reference to the decision to engage in exclusive or multiple relationships. If one or both partners are committed to the one-night stand, then being a good lover simply means having good technique, being sensitive to the wishes and feelings of the other, having the capacity to respond within the limits required by the other person, and similar technical considerations. But if one person will not have sex without knowing that there is a firm relationship, then frustration and retreat are likely to occur. For some, the opposite frame of mind holds. They do not wish to have a sense of obligation. Honest people will express their attitudes before they get undressed.

Then there's *consideration.* There are so many external circumstances which affect a person's sexuality. It is true that a larger proportion of men seem more sexually eager than women, but this is up to the point of encounter. Then the roles may become reversed or equalized. However, when a couple live together and do not have to engage in courtship rituals, they must have consideration for each other to a greater extent. An unmarried sexual pair can walk away from each other. Those who live together (with or without benefit of clergy) bear the consequences of their sexual acts and those circumstances which lead up to them. The man who insists on sex prematurely without arousing his partner is likely to leave her frustrated and angry with him. The woman who stays up till one o'clock to watch television, because the TV set and the only air conditioner are in the bedroom, succeeds in depriving her husband both of sleep and sex and does not make a friend.

The sense of uniqueness is required by many. It is a curiosity of human nature that the most intimate of experiences can also be thoroughly impersonal. I am not speaking about calling out the name of your second husband at a critical moment with your third. Nor that familiar slap on the fanny that used to tease a previous lover but outrages Ms. Current Lover. I mean the moment-by-moment awareness of the feelings of one's partner, with whatever changes of pace or personal expression are required to augment the experience and make the other person aware that you know he/she exists and matters. One is reminded of the lady who was in a bomb shelter during the V-bomb attack on London. She was complaining to her neighbor that she didn't like sex. When the latter remonstrated that she had four young children, she said, "Yes, I close my eyes and think of England."

I think that expressiveness is also part of being a good lover. Let your partner know what you feel, what you enjoy, even what you don't like or want changed. Since your enjoyment is vital to both of you, assuming that the relationship is really viable, you cannot ignore any possibility of letting your partner know how he/she can please you, provided you are willing to be pleased! If you are pleased, say so, encourage more sex, let the good spirits affect all parts of your relationship.

Finally, part of being a good lover is not being obnoxious. Reread the list of avoidable mistakes in the next chapter which would turn off the most loving, eager partner. If you can change by yourself, do so immediately. If you recognize your self-destructive attitudes in this list, you may need to get some psychotherapeutic consultation, because these characteristics will affect first your life in bed and then your life out of bed.

Self-destructive sexual games and harmful patterns make living with a particular person a miserable experience.

16) Sexual Games

Much of sexual self-destructiveness is perpetrated through initiating or being the victim of sexual games. I define a sexual game as an attempt to deceive the other person or oneself concerning one's real feelings and/or intentions through misleading or ambiguous words and actions. Since sex is potentially the most intense pleasure of life, this state of affairs seems to be ridiculous. Why should it be necessary for people who desire each other sexually to have to manipulate each other into a sexual relationship? The reason is very simple. Not only do individuals often act in their worst interests, but sex is also the carrier of feelings toward parents, self, society, and so forth. When you go to bed with somebody, there is an entire cast of characters in addition to the heroine and hero.

The nature of the seeming conflict between the sexes can be illustrated by these direct quotes:

HE: "The average unwed male would be doomed to celibacy if he didn't pretend a little bit."

SHE: "I want to get to know him as a person before we have sex."

Obviously, as long as there is the demand to get to know somebody, one has to run the risk that the data offered are tainted with selfish self-interest.

There are many purposes to sexual games, and several of them may be functioning simultaneously. Since most sexual games are the result of neurotic goals, distortions of reality, inability to relate, or psychopathic exploitation, one can easily see that to initiate them is to engage in self-destructiveness in one's personal life. Furthermore, it is vital to recognize these games so that one is not the victim of another person's destructiveness.

SOME GOALS OF SEXUAL GAMES

1. *Reducing vulnerability.* To ensure their emotional safety—that is, to avoid being hurt, rejected, or found inadequate—many people engage in amounts or patterns of sexuality which they would prefer not to. They relate sexually at once or not at all, or yield to sexual practices they dislike, to avoid having any confrontation that will reduce their feelings of self-esteem.

2. *Avoiding commitment.* At a given time, one may feel anxious at the idea of having a committed, exclusive relationship. Therefore his sexual behavior will be designed to keep his partner off balance and not expecting a continuing relationship.

3. *Setting up obligations.* To demonstrate the plasticity of sexual behavior and how it can be molded to meet quite extraneous considerations, we list this kind of manipulation next to avoiding commitment. To some women, the suggestion of sex becomes tantamount to a discussion of marriage. The slightest penetration is the equivalent of marriage vows. To break these vows is to become the victim of a great campaign of guilt-provocation.

4. *Attempting to deceive.* There is about as much outright lying in sex as there is in business. Probably more, since the laws of the states influence business procedures, but sexual behavior is generally limited only by one's imagination and childhood upbringing. People lie in order to conceal their feelings about the other person and their intentions. The forms of lying include false statements, social pressure, use of money and surroundings, and being more or less sexual than your body signals. Sexual exploitation is used for marriage, money, business, social contacts, good times, and entrée into particular circles.

5. *Attempting to control.* Since so many people regard sex as the emotional equivalent of their paycheck, they are subject to manipulative attempts at control. I remember a lady who once kissed me good night and told me that was my ration for the evening. I told myself that when kisses were rationed it was a disaster economy I didn't want to be a part of. This sort of iniq-

uity occurs within and without marriage, and women are generally the instigators. No person likes to feel that he or she must give this or that in order to have some sexual experience, so that the result is doubly self-destructive. First, the other person is resentful; second, you have deprived yourself of a good time.

6. *Inability to express feelings directly.* This is a serious problem when it occurs in the sexual area as in many others. Sometimes a relationship is not started because one person cannot tell the other person about the warmth he/she experiences. On the other hand, contacts can be continued indefinitely when no longer desired because "I don't want to hurt the other person's feelings." In either case, it is a game with both players losing.

7. *To bolster self-esteem.* Both men and women like to "score points." Lots of genital contact can become the means of assuaging parental criticism and teacher's lack of approval. Making orgasmic experience, or the lack of it, the way of compensating for the hurt feelings of twenty or more years earlier is only one more bit of evidence of the defectiveness of the human brain.

8. *For adventure.* Some people have a craving for excitement. The dullness of their lives causes them to want to step out on the town. It has no meaning except that it is more stimulating than the overall grayness of their existence. Obviously, unless there is a partner with the same minimal commitment of feelings, someone will be disappointed.

9. *Avoidance of loneliness.* If you are the type of person for whom loneliness is the worst of experiences, then sexuality or even marriage with unloved or disliked partners is your probable fate.

10. *Customary rituals.* It is interesting that even in the privacy of personal relationships people insist on following the requirements of convention. They take society to bed with them. It is expected that the man will try and the woman will resist. I have known women who spoke of their disappointment when the man didn't make a pass at them, even though they had no intention of having sex with him. Many men make their pitch as a matter of form, expecting neither acceptance nor ultimate satisfaction.

11. *Self-deception.* Sexual games are often entered into because the players cannot bear the thought of being unloved or

unloving. They are open to any kind of lie in order to tell themselves that they are attractive. The lie may be verbal, or it may consist of concealing from oneself that the behavior of the other person is harsh, inconsiderate, unloving, and generally indifferent to one's welfare.

To help you recognize specific sexual games, to break out of this neurotic pattern, and to defeat the intentions of others, I have listed some of the games under emotionally related categories.

SECURITY

1. *Ambiguity.* For this you set up a smokescreen in order not to reveal your true intentions. It is not clear whether or not you want sex, relate it to marriage, are interested in just having a date or in continuing the relationship.

2. *Giving.* This involves trying to entrap the other person through a sense of obligation. Lend your car, make lavish dinners, spend lots of money, and always listen to the tale of woe regardless of your mood.

3. *Instant sex.* To make sure that the other person won't run away, take off your clothes immediately. The futility of attempting to guarantee your lover's continued presence is obvious. I think that handcuffs would be better.

DECEPTION

1. *Outright lying.* Both men and women are capable of total distortions of their intentions, backgrounds, finances, and everything else important in order to obtain or avert the possibility of sexual relations. There is no guarantee that you won't be taken in. If in doubt, ask questions. If you are deceived, refuse to see the person again. A liar will damage you in more ways than sexual deceit.

2. *Going out with an impossible person.* Some people will form temporary relationships for self-convenience. They know quite well that they will never marry or form a deep relationship with their partner for reasons of age, religion, finances, appearance, and so on. They will cheerfully permit the other person to develop deep feelings based on false appearances so

that they will temporarily have a partner, either until their circumstances improve or until somebody better comes along. The only defense for the patsy is to try to get the other person to express himself as clearly as possible. Ask questions, stop talking, and listen. Yes, I said stop talking. Shut your mouth and listen. If your lover is close-mouthed, he/she may have a reason for not giving himself away.

3. *Pretending to have feelings.* This little game is meant to preserve one's own ego, not necessarily to damage the other person. I have a patient who for a period of ten months did not reveal to her lover that she wasn't having an orgasm. Stating this is harder later than sooner. This kind of behavior is obviously designed to keep a weak relationship going for fear that it will collapse when the partner realizes that there are limits to his lover's responsiveness.

4. *Playing a false role.* Individuals pretend to be stronger or weaker than they are in order to entice the other person, or give the kind of impression they think is desired. I know of one woman who often took the initiative in a relationship until it came to paying the bill. In this kind of situation some men are likely to pay for only their own share and then walk out. To play the role of being strong is particularly self-destructive. The other person becomes far too dependent. Then, when your own feelings of weakness require you to stop giving or, God forbid, even to ask for help, you are met with expressions of disbelief and even rage. "I thought you were so strong."

TRANSFERENCE

1. *Attributing false positive qualities.* Sometimes we expect that a person with trivial similarities to our parents will continue to treat us in the same way as our parents did when we were children. A partner like the strong father or warm mother is a good example. Unfortunately, the partner may have similar expectations of exceptional treatment, and that's where the conflict and frustration begin.

2. *Attributing false negative qualities.* We can just as easily exaggerate the meaning of various unpleasant qualities because they are reminiscent of how somebody else treated us. A woman once said to me, after I had spent a quiet Saturday evening

with some friends in her company after an exhausting six-day week, "You are just like my ex-husband. He always was passive." She KO'd herself.

3. *Falling in love with cold, indifferent people.* This is an attempt to obtain vindication for childhood feelings of rejection. We select somebody with some slight resemblance to our parents, somebody who very likely has no warm feelings for us. Then, because of their very coldness, we try to make them love us just as we would have wanted our parents to love us.

4. *Sado-masochism.* This is a very complicated lifestyle between two partners in which one plays the role of aggressor while the other plays victim. It frequently evolves from illtreatment when one was young, fantasies of revenge and of having a very good parent, and liberal quantities of self-deception as to how it really was.

CHILDHOOD FANTASIES

1. *Brünnhilde.* Some children have exaggerated feelings about their own worth. When they grow up they expect their mate to prove himself/herself just as the Norse hero Siegfried had to go through the magic fire in order to rescue the sleeping Brünnhilde from her rock.

2. *Sleeping Beauty.* A closely related fantasy is the need to be recognized as exceptionally valuable, even, for example, as the prince was able to see the virtues of the Sleeping Beauty while she was asleep.

3. *The Princess.* This is a form of sexual game in which the player, not always a woman, demands special treatment in return for sex. The gift of one's body on an exclusive, legal basis is considered to be so great that the recipient is considered to be obligated on a lifelong basis to revere, spoil, and behave subordinately.

4. *Don Juan.* Although named after a gentleman, this form of self-destructiveness is not exclusively male. The basic fantasy is that there is some partner who can satisfy all of one's needs. As a result, there is no tolerance for the frailties of one's present sexual partner. The experience of imperfection or lack of total gratification leads to the immediate severing of the relationship and the quest for someone new who will not be disappointing.

5. *Rebelliousness*. Selecting a partner of whom parents would disapprove is a terribly poor way of selecting a mate. It implies that one's values are significantly different from those of one's parents. Unfortunately, the mate frequently turns out to be a carbon copy of one parent. You may then find that you have not rejected your parental household as much as you think.

AVOIDING SELF-DESTRUCTIVENESS

Games and other sexually self-destructive behavior are frequently exceptionally difficult to change. One reason is the amount of short-term gratification obtained from sex. The psychologists who have studied how people learn state that behavior which accompanied some pleasure is likely to be repeated. As a result, self-destructive sexual behavior will also be repeated even if it violates emotional common sense. Therefore sexual attitudes that are hurtful to one's partner, or are counterproductive in achieving one's own valued lifestyle, are reluctantly given up if they offer even slight or occasional pleasure.

How, then, can you change your sexual attitudes and behavior? Part of the solution is to have a clear alternative. Then, as you are confronted with choices and decisions, you can ask yourself whether the results will be consistent with some larger life plan. It is likely that there will be deviations from plan, but if you have confidence that you want to change, and resolutely refuse to add to your emotional discomfort in the form of doubt, then you will be able to improve your lifestyle.

MISTAKES MAKING MATES MISERABLE

There are harmful patterns which make living with a particular person a miserable experience. Check yourself out to see if you make any of these mistakes.

1. *Nagging*. Learn to take no for an answer. In some states it is legal to assault nags physically. They deserve it.

2. *Abusiveness*. To curse and emphasize the weaknesses and faults of a mate, or to exaggerate criticism in any way, is to destroy the other partner's good feelings for you. Abuse is often remembered longer than kind words.

3. *Permitting mistreatment.* By letting yourself be abused, exploited, or otherwise mistreated, you ruin your own good spirits, set a poor model for your children, and make your mate feel guilty. He will then continue to abuse you until you stop him by punishing him. Stop the vicious circle immediately. Call the police if necessary.

4. *Possessiveness.* If you are overly controlling and stifle your partner, you will end up married to an uninteresting, sniveling, resentful dishrag. Then, when you complain to your buddies or the bridge club about what an uninteresting, passive, dependent mate you have, the only honest answer will be that you created your own dissatisfaction.

5. *Living through the other party.* Do your own thing. Then if your partner fails, it is his failure and you can reassure him. The last thing you want to do is to attack somebody for failing or for slowing down, feeling that it becomes your personal failure. This is the road to being hated.

6. *Demanding that the partner match our ideals.* You are probably sufficiently confused to have difficulty running your own affairs with emotional common sense. Where do you get off setting standards for other people?

7. *Showing passiveness and evading responsibility.* To let your resources atrophy and to be reliant excessively on the other party is to reduce the quality of your own life, because then only one brain and pair of hands are at work. It is also an invitation to be treated with contempt and to be ignored when decisions are made.

8. *Excessive ties with parents.* Nobody knows better than you how you were mistreated when you were at home and about the problems your parents had in running their lives with rationality and compassion toward each other. To insist that they be taken into consideration in the decision making now only means that you are still an obedient child. Make your own mistakes.

9. *Using sex as reward and punishment.* Sex should not be contingent on the good behavior of your partner. The central nervous system does not react kindly to having sexual experiences associated with conflicts, anger, and frustration. If you take your anger to bed, you will also have as bed partners two

lawyers, two accountants, and a judge. Watching carefully will be your children, the neighbors, and your parents.

10. *Provoking a fight as a test of love.* This is a sign of a serious personality disturbance. Anybody who feels that only a loving person will fight with him is nuts. It shows that he lacks influence over the other person and cannot express his anger and love directly. You can certainly make a situation worse and lose your partner unexpectedly with this foolish tactic.

11. *Getting the last word.* There are more important issues in life than who is right or wrong. I have had the opportunity as a psychotherapist to hear about fights over such vital issues as when to put the butter away, whether cremation is a satisfactory way of disposing of a body, and so on. Express your feelings calmly, insist that the other person respect your right to have an opinion, then shut up. (Refer back to paragraph 1, Nagging.)

12. *Competitiveness.* Do your own thing. Remember that when you are competitive with your partner it is somebody you love whom you are defeating.

13. *Interrupting.* Not to let the other person express his/her feelings or to finish a thought is highly irritating. It points to a lack of consideration of the other person's feelings and a dominating attitude. Have no doubts, you will be treated accordingly.

14. *Holding back your feelings.* As we have noted repeatedly, this affects your own spirits and must have a deleterious effect on the relationship. Let the other person know of your love and your anger and your dependency. But do this in a way that the message can be heard.

15. *Expecting total satisfaction.* This is the royal road to unhappiness. It guarantees that you will be not only frustrated but will find it necessary to demand and intimidate others to get what you believe is coming to you. You will achieve not satisfaction but fury.

At this point I have reviewed many of the self-destructive ways in which people act—toward their mates and other members of their family, in business, and so on. I believe that through self-understanding, and with some self-discipline, you can improve the quality of your life by following these guidelines.

If there are particular problem areas which you feel are beyond your own capacity to deal with, it would be self-destructive to suffer unnecessarily. You should then try to get psychotherapeutic assistance. Chapter 20 offers help in choosing a therapist.

17) Fear of Success

There is no greater evidence of our self-destructive qualities than the price people pay for sabotaging their successes. One would think that the vision of life passing by and problems building up would be enough to spur us into constructive action. Sometimes, we can seemingly be about to achieve our dreams, only to blow our achievement out of the water! Examination of the reasons why people do not make progress toward constructive goals reveals that all of the emotional discomforts we have been discussing play their role, plus a few more.

Fear of success is a belief that achieving what we really want would cause such emotional distress that the price is too much to pay. To be successful is to be upset. That's logical (?).

COMPETENCE AND INCOMPETENCE

Inability to make progress toward goals, feeling incompetent, and not wanting to master situations—generally all these have their origins in childhood. Most children are prepared to demand help, to accept, not to feel guilty about it, and then to respond in an affectionate way toward their parents. As we mature, most of us explore and learn a great deal about our world. Some of us, it is true, come into the world hampered by excessive timidity and anxiety. In these cases it is the task of our parents to give us support so that normal development and maturation occurs. One typical milestone is the first day of school. Some of us fight like hell against entry into the wide world. Others enjoy getting lost there, and report home only in time for the late show. Do you remember your own early experiences of school? Do they reveal a child who was curious and confident, or entangled in those famous apron strings? A crippling mood such as feelings of incompetence evolves from parents' desire for obedience, a need to have their child conform to family or community expectations, and displacement of their anger with each other onto the kid. Some parents have a strong desire that the child remain dependent, express himself/herself in particular ways, and be a butt for their own hostility and insecurity. The *courageous child* is not given guidance on how to develop a sense of mastery and competence in dealing with the world, support for failure, or instruction in how to cope with new situations. The *fearful child* is not gently urged toward achievement, with the belief that the cost of failure is not so great so long as a loving home is available as a secure nest.

As children we are sensitive to parental expectations because of our vulnerability. There are studies of children that show that they literally become depressed and then die, even in the presence of good physical care, if some personal touch is lacking. Children are vulnerable when the parents withhold approval and become punitive, abusive, or critical. Simultaneously, this kind of manipulation also makes us angry. If anger is encouraged as legitimate, or if we are abused or ignored, it has a profound influence upon our personality. The attitude of our parents toward success and the outside world programs us in ways of accomplishing tasks. However, too frequently it is couched in mixed messages encouraging both effort and fear, or perhaps one parent views the world one way and the other has a contradictory or different philosophy of action.

Style of achieving our goals. This is influenced by how affection and approval were supplied, whether anger was restrained or cruel, the wisdom or foolishness of what we were taught about life, and how much support we got when the inevitable abrasions of the outside world begin to wear down on us. We experience life, have deep feelings, develop an identification, draw conclusions which shape our philosophy, and ultimately see ourselves as more or less *competent*. A sense of competence is surely the greatest help to leading a life free of routine and degradation. After all, when we say to ourselves that we can master whatever tasks lead toward our goals, then we will refuse to put up with poor jobs, degrading marriages, and so forth. When we inform ourselves that we are incompetent, then we take no risks that will rock the boat. Moreover, goals can be selected which are realistic and designed to improve one's situation.

GOALS

The likelihood of success is related to the nature of one's goals. Alfred Adler pointed out very clearly that the sense of inadequacy so many of us experience as children is compensated for by devising the goal of being superior in some way. Obviously, the child can predict neither his personality nor his life situation decades in advance. Consequently, a goal originating in childhood, designed to overcome juvenile emotional discomforts, is going to lead us wide of the mark as we take on adult responsibilities, roles, and opportunities. This will be particularly true if we are unfortunate enough to have developed a goal of such power, glory, riches, or beauty as to be either unattainable or excessively costly.

Frequently goals are neither an appropriate extension of our identity nor a natural development of our personality. One should be careful not to make the mistake of assuming that overcoming weakness and becoming prominent is a neurotic goal bound to fail. I suspect that if one were to study the careers of the Teddy Roosevelts (sickly child) and Beethovens (abused by a drunken father and later deaf) in the world, one would see that they had a shrewd estimate of their own capabilities. Moreover, they were *hard-working, capable of risks,* and *willing to undergo plenty of self-sacrifice.*

HOW PEOPLE DEFINE SUCCESS

On several occasions, I have asked groups of people to define what success meant to them at their stage of life. A variety of experiences and hopes were expressed. Success is as individually defined as values and beauty. I have summarized some of the ways that people define success:

Using other's standards. Sometimes it's our parents' values, and sometimes those of "society," but some of us do not define success in terms of our own potentialities.

A woman said, "My oldest brother used to terrorize my mother, while nothing I did was good enough for my father. I was awful at the piano. I got nervous when my father would yell, 'You made a mistake.' Even when I did well in a 'crap course' my hand froze. I've learned not to let other people define what success is. I learned to say 'ouch.' It hurts to define yourself as a hunk of garbage. One friend told me to act the way she wanted me to act. I don't want crumbs. I want my own identity. I renew friendships with those I feel good with." It was a struggle to overcome childhood anticipation of emotional brutality, but her standards are healthy.

Getting approval. Affirmation from peers or parents is important to some. "I wanted my father to be proud of me. His face is before me when I make a decision. I consider my children in every decision. Although both of my parents are dead, they are with me in every major decision."

Better mood. People spoke about feeling good, achieving peace of mind, being happy, doing what is interesting, getting what they want (not too late), and being able to cope with most problems:

"I want a positive framework for my life, not a depressed, oppressive one. A positive outlook. I become mired in an attitude which is not what I want to confront my life with."

Personal development. By this people mean getting the most from their potential, becoming more self-assertive, realizing meaningful goals, asking for what they want, achieving emotional independence, losing weight, and so forth.

A woman told me, "I've done some good things. [At which point she felt fear and anguish.] I don't believe it. I'm so conditioned to believe the opposite that to affirm it is some sort of betrayal of my father. I don't understand what makes it so hurtful. There is some conflict I'm wrestling with. I don't fight my battles. I'm going to get rid of my own criticism. This is making me dizzy. [After a while.] My strength is coming back. There will be forward motion. Ultimately it's guts, raw nerve. Receiving, accepting, and embracing reality. Moving away from self-conscious feelings. Taking my life seriously and realizing that it is up to me. [I told her that obviously her work was important and somebody was making profit from her.] I will not put myself into second-class situations." For her, the development of self-assertion and seeing herself as important was a struggle so important that she had bodily symptoms as though she were in a long battle.

Relationships. To have a personal relationship, i.e., a good marriage, or a long-term relationship with one person, is the goal of many of us. Some define this in terms of having children, or being a good wife or husband.

During a therapy session with a woman, I raised the issue of the resemblance between her relationship to her father, and the way she saw the company she worked for. She told me of a dream in which her father was unreliable. He wanted children but didn't want anybody to cling to him. He alternated between being warm and being unsupporting when she was in trouble. She developed the idea that men couldn't be trusted to be on her team. Reaching out to a lawyer friend for help with an employment problem was a step forward in developing the capacity for trust.

Achievement. This is the most common concept of success and is defined in a great variety of ways—from defining a career or job goal, through changing a job, to writing a great work of philosophy and promulgating one's ideas!

THE EMOTIONAL COMMON SENSE DEFINITION OF SUCCESS

We have seen that success can be applicable to all personal areas of importance, e.g., creativity, careers, personal life, and emotional development. The kind of success that will be most fulfilling evolves from your identity. When you experience some of your qualities very distinctly, you will enjoy either *expressing them* (the positive ones) or *overcoming them* (the negative ones). To be successful is to win your own battles, not those selected by your parents or some impersonal force such as "society."

Success can only be defined in terms of rewards (defined by our own values) for achieving personal goals. It is worth repeating: It is empty, valueless, and frustrating to define success in terms of standards other people set for us. The most that can be gained is some degree of approval, or perhaps avoiding criticism. The autonomous person has achieved some independence of other people's expectations. The person whose successes are defined by other people, and whose rewards are their approval, has not matured emotionally from the crib.

Why don't you reread the material on identity (Chapter 1), specifically whether you would rate yourself a Victim or a Victor, a Masochist or an Optimist. You will be able to utilize this material to help you to understand whether you have been sabotaging your own success.

FEAR OF SUCCESS

Why do so many of us collapse emotionally just when it appears that we have reached what we have sought at the cost of so much time and effort. To be successful means entering another category, achieving a new lifestyle. Anticipating these changes charges up our identification nuclei. Some of these have been resting and waiting for a chance to jab at our psyche with such feelings as *dependency, unworthiness, hostility, anxiety, rebelliousness,* and *need for approval.* These lead to sufficient disorganization to ruin the opportunity of succeeding with an important project.

Avoiding competition with parents. Here is how one man put it: "I do everything to avoid success. My father was a competitive parent. It took the form of disparaging my achievements as a child. It left me with an enduring sense of lack of competence relative to my abilities. I am full of anxiety. I satisfy myself with less than my full potential when success is imminent. I have a real fear of achieving my goals. I purposely fail to properly define them in order to keep a distance from achieving them. As my awareness of this strategy has grown, I've gotten closer to a solution to my problem. *My anxiety is increasing.* I have a vested interest in self-destruction. I remember the parental instruction to remain in the shadow of my father. I am relatively comfortable in a situation where I am not risking anything, i.e., unimportant areas. I avoid anxiety by not putting myself on the line." This adult still believes that his father is in a position to define his sense of value.

Separation anxiety. For some, achieving success means self-transformation into a new kind of creature that is no longer a member of the old loving, supporting, encouraging family that (never) existed. To succeed means to totally reject their parents. In their minds, they are snobs, or even worse, they are thumbing their noses at old Ma and Pa. In their minds, the childhood fantasy of superiority has been tied up, just waiting for a chance to sprint out: "When I grow up, I will show you. I won't need you. I am so angry with you that I will humiliate you by demonstrating how wrong you were in your doubts and mistreatment." Thus, to succeed is to not only prove that parents or teacher or older brother or younger sister were wrong, but it is an unforgivable act of hostility to be avoided. Why? Because some people have the delusion as adults that they still need Ma and Pa's approval, and they will have to creep into a hole if they give up all hope—unto Eternity—of getting that nice pat on the head: "You dear, sweet child, I knew all along that a talented, lovable offspring of mine would really make me proud and offer a truly marvelous contribution to the welfare of the entire world."

A woman said, "Fear of not succeeding became overwhelming to me. *The idea of not attaining success is paralyzing.* I attach too much importance to succeeding. Parents always mean well. [A way of denying their hostility.] My father was impossible to please, nothing was good enough. If I didn't find something, he would say, 'How stupid can you be?' I was an excellent student with a ninety-six average. 'Very good, but you can do better.' I was outraged, but they thought it was encouraging. It's a paralyzing thought to go after success. [To succeed or not to succeed is disorganizing.] "I put effort into my goal and not to achieve it would be devastating. I would be a complete failure. If I had a doctorate, I could say to my father, 'I was a success. See, you *were completely wrong.*' 'Girls shouldn't be successful,' my father thought. Yet he wanted me to have higher marks. I couldn't skip grades, because it would give my father a complex." With such mixed messages, one cannot know where the road lies to emotional fulfillment.

Tec (1976) has offered additional insights into fear of success. He asserts that we may feel *unworthy,* i.e., have the unconscious fear that the success is not justified and that we are a fraud. To be number one requires that one prove one's worthiness. Moreover, success might arouse resentment (causing loss of one's colleagues' emotional support), or interference with other aspects of our life, e.g., marriage. Winning can be nerve-racking, because it is at somebody's expense and we will lose their emotional support. Moreover, if a promotion or new assignment calls for a radically different style of behavior, or new skills, the old habits of performance may not be useful in the new position. Insecurity can keep one from making serious attempts to master new tasks.

Perhaps we feel unentitled to the goodies of life: "I used to think that Bloomingdale's wasn't for me. My parents didn't educate me about the value of money and how earning it made it one's own to spend. I used to feel comfortable buying only at such stores as "X" and "Y," where people would buy who were earning less than I." This is an example of how reaching the lifestyle of the more successful person raises anxiety which discourages further achievement.

THE EMOTIONAL COMMON SENSE APPROACH TO GOALS

You will start to gain control over your life by deciding what you want from it. What are your goals? What is it that you really want in life?

GOAL QUESTIONNAIRE

My personal goals.

1.

2.

3.

4.

5.

Now think about your goals. Then answer these questions:

1. Are they my goals for me, or did somebody else set them up for me?
2. Are they reasonable? Do I have the intellectual, temperamental, monetary, and other resources to reach them?
3. How long will it take to get there?
4. Do I care to invest that amount of time?

5. How old will I be when I have reached my goals, and how much time will I have to enjoy them?
6. Have I thought about my values in life, i.e., what I feel deeply about and what repels me?
7. Are my goals consistent with these values? Do my values add energy to achieving my goals, or will they create internal conflicts?
8. Can I achieve my goals through activities which I enjoy?
9. Am I willing to make the sacrifices to reach these goals?
10. Are my standards realistic, i.e., will I be satisfied with the results of what I can achieve?

Priorities. If I am to achieve these goals, what actions must I take, i.e., what are my priorities? What must I do first, even if other things remain undone?

1.

2.

3.

4.

5.

Who are the people in my life who will help me achieve my goals?

1.

2.

3.

4.

5.

What people are hindrances to my achieving my goals?

1.

2.

3.

4.

5.

18) Emotional Problems of Employment

One's job is frequently the most serious cause of stress and emotional disorders. In this chapter, we will explore two ideas:

• What is the emotional common sense approach to employment?

• How do you judge whether a job is or is not suitable?

Read this material with care! You may come to the conclusion that you will have to fire your supervisor (quit)!

The Marxists among you may cry out that employment problems are all due to the System: To them I say: (1) Baloney; (2) Keep on reading.

It is perfectly true that there are vast inequities in our system. Some years ago I was personally on an unemployment line and disqualified because I earned a measly few bucks in my private practice. No matter that my employer was a thief who stole from his clients, his workers, and the government. I didn't stay around while he didn't pay my fees. I quit. In fact, I won a judgment against him and found it impossible to collect, though my lawyers made out quite nicely. I tell you this to show that I haven't been living in an ivory tower.

EMPLOYMENT STRESS

The chief source of employment stress is a mismatch between the worker and the position. This occurs for a variety of reasons:

• *Those responsible for recruiting and hiring do not know what they are doing.* They understand neither the position nor the intangible qualities of the organization that contribute to success and failure.

• *People who look for jobs don't know what they are doing.* Lacking self-understanding they either take the first position offered or accept positions that demand qualities of personality and work style that they cannot provide.

DIMENSIONS OF JOB SUITABILITY

My experience in career development, interviews with personnel directors of major organizations, and reading news reports of personnel changes and product successes and failures, suggest that the following are some of the considerations which contribute to success or failure. Most of them are *intangible factors,* i.e., subjective ways of reacting to situations which are independent of actual skill (except for paragraph 1). Most people succeed or fail because of reasons other than independent actual competence. It is the intangible qualities of style and way of handling problems and people that make the difference!

1. Technical. The up-to-date skills and resources necessary to solve problems and understand new developments.

2. Style. These are the usual ways that people handle problems and people, i.e., their easily recognizable qualities that distinguish them from other people, even those with the same job title:

• *Cosmetic.* One's appearance, behavior, and social and economic background which are regarded favorably or unfavorably by one's supervisors and colleagues.

• *Cognitive.* How one approaches technical situations and problems. People have different preferences and abilities in the levels of abstraction and degree of complexity of the tasks they can do well.

• *Social.* Techniques and habits of dealing with people, and dealing with one's own and others' hostility, dependency, authority, and need for content.

• *Motivational.* How one deals with insecurity, need for power, and perception of the organization and one's particular role in the organization.

• *Psychological stamina.* How one deals with unpleasant information, i.e., possibility of failure, ethical conflicts, opposition, and need for delay in making decisions.

3. Locus. What size of company or department do you prefer, e.g., large or intimate? What region of the country do you prefer, e.g., urban or suburban?

4. Level and nature of application. Do you prefer to be a manager, scientist, technician, or staff person?

5. Benefits. What are the pay, perquisites, prestige, retirement benefits, and stock options?

6. Identification. What values, goals, and self-image are required (or do you possess)? For example, a *New York Times* article (Wareham, 1979) described the values emphasized in corporations as conformity, savoir-faire, tolerance, willingness to compromise, and moderation.

7. Motivation. The desire for excellence and productivity.

8. Wish to continue developing. Desire for continued maturation.

9. Health and stamina. Personal resources to continue functioning under adverse circumstances.

10. Flexibility. The ability to deal with varied and unexpected events.

11. Family and personal requirements. What is needed and/or available from one's family, in terms of emotional support, economic needs, and requirements for a parent's presence.

EMOTIONAL PROBLEMS COMMON AT WORK

Your job can stir up a wide variety of stresses and emotional disorders: alcoholism, gain or loss of weight, drug abuse, depression, irritability, conflicts, tension, preoccupation with extraneous ideas, racing thoughts, psychosis, withdrawal, passivity, and such physical ailments as headaches, arthritis, ulcers, high blood pressure, heart attacks, palpitations, low blood sugar, digestive problems, sleep disturbance, muscle tension, restlessness, perspiration, cold hands, and sexual problems.

How do you know that these problems come from work? Do you show absenteeism, lateness, feeling like quitting, dissatisfaction, accidents, withdrawal from your colleagues, bursts of social contact, or such lapses of efficiency as poor memory, poor judgment, reduced ability to take risks, excessive riskiness, carelessness, avoidance of problems?

Why do people drive others nutty on the job? Frequent themes people have told me about include:

- *Vindication.* "I will show people that I am successful, not a failure."
- *Revenge.* "I was pushed around when I was little. Now it is my turn."
- *Acceptance.* "If I show what a nice guy I am, I will be liked."
- *Achievement.* "Being useful gives me a sense of value."
- *Power.* "If I am strong, nobody can push me around."
- *Self-contempt.* "I have to be Mr. Big, to hide the hurt child in me."
- *Pleasing old Dad.* "Pop won't like me unless I am a success."

All of these motives (conscious and unconscious) are hidden agendas which create demands upon one's associates at all levels. They frequently are counterproductive so far as productivity and personal satisfaction are concerned. Therefore, if a supervisor or colleague is motivated in some of the ways listed above, you are under pressure to act in ways which you can't understand to meet the emotional needs of somebody who may not reward you appropriately.

Adjustment to a job. This involves not only your skills and personality characteristics as a worker but how you relate to the peculiarities of a particular position and what nonemployment factors influence your life. The transportation available to you and your family may play as important a role in your adjustment as your skills or the qualities of your supervisor. To select a career, or even a position, or to evaluate why you are uptight every day at the plant, requires as comprehensive a personal diagnosis as why you can't get along with your spouse or lover. Most people just grouse about it and do not make any changes which would improve their peace of mind.

Key areas of vocational adjustment overlap considerably with other seemingly more personal problems. However, there is one difference which has been repeatedly reported to me. Many people complain that the area of business is more dishonest than other areas of life. I personally found that there was more lying and cheating in a brief sojourn that I had made into a particular area of the business world than in over a decade of work in various institutions and colleges. What are some examples?

I know a salesman who dislikes the need always to be cheerful with his accounts. As he puts it, "I can't be myself." Other people feel that they cannot get honest appraisals of their work because of insecure supervisors. Another instance is the requirement to put in one's best efforts, even though there is a lack of identification with the company's product, or services, or the values which are represented.

Supervision. Supervisory and management failure is one of the most costly social problems in this country. The reasons some people are promoted is not their love for excellence and capacity to perform supervisory duties. Supervisors are often promoted, transferred, or fired because of favoritism, company politics, and acquisition by other businesses. Incompetents arc often protected because to discharge them would be to admit error, or to acknowledge criminally selfish union policies, or to say that their work is really done by others. The consequence is high prices, company failures, product dangers and inadequacies, and loss of employment.

The most familiar complaint is the arrogant attitude of supervisors. I remember that when I was a young psychologist working in state hospitals, the directors were known for their ruthlessness. People were fired for walking on the grass and instructed to live on hospital grounds when they owned homes in a nearby town. Most of the comfortable quarters in the hospital were changed to offices. These so-called psychiatrists had come up through the system and instead of learning compassion in dealing with their fellow employees had waited until they reached the top to compensate by heaping vengeance on subordinates. There are many supervisors who scream, derogate, keep creative people from flourishing, devise or implement petty, tyrannical regulations, or are indifferent to the working conditions, wages, and spirits of those whose economic welfare has been entrusted to them. Many of these individuals at high levels look the other way when their subordinates mistreat those under them.

Some supervisors are afraid to take any risks. They reject

good suggestions or requests for compassionate personnel action because of fear that their own supervisors will turn them down. Their fear of assuming authority causes them to look elsewhere when the genuinely disruptive employee interferes with the capacity of others to work through noise, non-cooperation and bullying. Sometimes they sabotage others' creative efforts by keeping outdated procedures and hiring or promoting incompetents.

Do not misunderstand my remarks about supervisors to mean that I am opposed to authority. A healthy technological society depends on some individuals assuming a great deal of responsibility and authority. What I am referring to is the *misuse of authority*. It is also true that many employees are deliberately negligent, lackadaisical, or even saboteurs! At all levels people can spoil an organization's efficiency.

FOUR BASIC ROLES

These are *assertion, compliance, indecisiveness, and rebelliousness* (Piotrowski, 1957). The reader ought to consider his own attitude toward supervisors, colleagues, and subordinates. If you find yourself always assuming an authoritarian know-it-all approach to the people you deal with, then it is likely that you are either arrogant or rebellious. You are transferring the superior attitude inculcated in you as a child or developed by you in defense against feelings of worthlessness. On the other hand, if you are uncomfortable in exercising authority—e.g., giving orders, correcting mistakes, maintaining discipline, firing goof-offs—then you feel unworthy of assuming responsibility. You must either develop self-confidence or move to a position that does not feed these feelings of inadequacy. But don't stay there and suffer or cause others to suffer. Perhaps you can develop new qualities of leadership and self-assertion.

Insecurity. It is possible to be talented and productive and yet feel that one is performing inadequately. The ideas of personal worth and vocational success are frequently mixed up. The child who is raised to feel valueless carries this self-image to school and job. Conversely, a failure at school or work may mean to the person that he is really no good. Since low self-esteem reduces likelihood of success, a cycle arises of discouragement, hopelessness, and then genuine lack of progress or outright failure.

Discrimination. Our country is notorious for this. In turn the Italians, Irish, Jews, blacks, and Puerto Ricans have suffered from it. I know one nonJew who was discriminated against because he looked like a Jew.

What about discrimination against women? There is no doubt that women still find it harder than men do to get into some technical schools and to obtain responsible positions and advancement in many industries and particular companies. In part, the prejudice against promoting women is the small child's resentment against his mother and teachers. However, the excessive struggle for women to achieve success as well as the social pressures which cause them to seek lower goals create personality problems which add to the normal difficulties of being a competent supervisor. The only answer is to insist that all promotions be based on talent. The implication is that some women, some members of minority groups or any others really might not have the personality to be promoted. But it is self-destructive to prevent those who are technically and emotionally competent people from getting ahead. Eventually, every individual would be encouraged to develop his talents and could plan on increasing his responsibilities without fear or frustration due to prejudice.

The meaningfulness of work. It is commonplace that the need for craftsmanship and for individual skills has been so reduced as to create a serious mental-hygiene problem. There are enormous numbers of repetitive service positions like sorting letters, selling stamps or subway tokens, punching computer data cards, and filing correspondence. Workers on automated motorcar assembly lines go berserk or deliberately sabotage vehicles in order to obtain some excitement. Many of the people filling these jobs have the intelligence and emotional stamina to handle more complex, demanding positions. Even in large organizations whose functions have high social value, the proportion of tedious, routinized jobs is very large. Some people respond to boredom with depression. Busy work is sometimes created to justify the empire-building of dishonest managers.

Most people want some degree of recognition. They want to be praised, to receive economic and emotional rewards for their services. However, this is sometimes a frustrating trap. Recognition may be sought not as a personal reward but as a vindication. Recognition means that parents were wrong in telling you that you would never be a success, that your wife is wrong in thinking you a failure, or that your children will consider you a hero. A normal degree of hope for success and esteem can also be frustrated by the routine nature of one's position or the negativistic attitudes of jealous supervisors.

THE EMOTIONAL COMMON SENSE APPROACH TO EMPLOYMENT

1. *Do not expect justice.* There are many factors which go into success. Hard work and talent are only two of them. You should be prepared to experience favoritism, arrogance, cowardice, lying, broken promises, illegal activities, being stabbed in the back, bad luck, poor timing, difficult economic conditions, and many other mishaps.

2. *Be prepared to work hard.* Earn a honest day's pay. If you have genuine reason to be dissatisfied, emotional common sense requires that you not be a patsy forever, and you must be prepared to change jobs or get a transfer. Therefore you must be able to convince your new employer, either with or without a reference, that you are a capable worker and interested in producing, regardless of personal discomfort. Work, but look around.

3. *Know your own talents and capacities.* There are characteristics you have that will be natural for some jobs and render you uncomfortable or cause you to bomb out on others. Professional guidance from a vocational or industrial psychologist might be helpful.

4. *Be yourself.* Whether you are a salesman, a clerk, a manager, or a professional person, you have a style of living which can be expressed on a job and which makes you comfortable and doesn't antagonize others. If you believe that you are required to be excessively compliant, be more forthright. If the supervisors or clientele with whom you deal require a hypocritical, plastic manner and this is not you, then consider whether you are in the wrong occupation or with the wrong firm.

5. *Don't let yourself be bullied or abused.* Always remember that many of your supervisors have been appointed to their positions or have wheedled their way there not because they are competent but rather because they are acting out infantile feelings of inferiority. Therefore, should you find yourself in a position in which you are being pushed around needlessly, then fight back. You will rarely be fired, and if so it will be worth it. Many individuals suffer from neurotic feelings of guilt. They feel better when limits are placed on their hostility. Do not get into a neurotic guilt-provocation–punishment cycle. You must preserve your self-respect and not have the remainder of your day and free time ruined because of rumination over being abused. If you know your organization you may be able to call the situation to somebody's attention discreetly and in a constructive way. If you try and fail, then you must either fight or run. Remember the Chinese proverb already mentioned: "Of the thirty-six ways of averting disaster, running away is best." Do not let your head hang in the noose.

6. *Show initiative.* It is not terrible to have a suggestion refused or a request not granted. Try to put your imprint on your department. If you cannot do so, then you ought to take stock. Perhaps your ideas are less effective than you believe. In this case, you require more experience or education. However, if this is not the case, prepare yourself for a new organization which can use some fresh blood.

7. *Keep your education up to date.* If you are resigned to tedious, repetitive jobs, getting your jollies only in your free time, then skip to the next section. Nothing gets out of date faster than knowledge. Participate in in-service training conscientiously. If this is not available, then you must make the sacrifice to study at home or at an institution. If you cannot bear to tear yourself away from golf, tennis, the kiddies, or that number you've been courting, then the price you pay will be very precise. Your career will slow down, and people no more competent than you will get ahead and earn more money and have fewer frustrations in the professional area.

8. *Be an effective leader.* I learned an invaluable idea in ROTC. A leader performs two functions simultaneously: He performs the mission, and he looks out for the welfare of his men. If you believe that you can drive the slaves under you or

look out for your own interests without reference to your subordinates' welfare, you may possibly succeed. But your future is
also limited. You may go nowhere because your staff will perform in ways that do you no credit. You are probably stuck in
your current job forever. Further, you will live forty hours a
week in an environment in which you are despised. I have had
supervisors who drove the staff while spending their own time
reading cheap novels (feet up on the radiator) or contacting
their stockbrokers. Had their own supervisors taken an interest
in the effectiveness of their department, these people would
have been fired or forced to be productive. Instead, I chose to
leave, because my own well-being forbade me to be exploited
by these selfish incompetents.

9. *Be courageous.* As I pointed out before, it is generally wise
to fight back if you are bullied. What some people use as a
guide are statements like this to their supervisors: "Fire me, but
don't abuse me; fire me or trust me." I had the chief of a clinic
who was on an on-time kick call me in and ask me where I was
at eight o'clock that morning. I looked him in the eye and asked
him where he had been at four-thirty yesterday. He went
screaming to my immediate chief and complained about my attitude, but he never asked me again what time I arrived. *He
knew I was watching him.* Confront the bully. As one person
put it, "What's more important—the dollars or how you feel?" If
you feel discriminated against, then the first thing to do is to
determine whether your efforts and the quality of your work
really warrant a promotion or raise. If they do, then ask for it.
Finally, if necessary, go to the appropriate governmental agency
and demand that the laws be enforced. After all, there may be
some young, energetic, hungry fellow there just aching to make
a name for himself through helping a deserving person like you
against that monstrous corporation.

10. *Blow your own horn.* If you want recognition, let people
know what you have done. Better yet, make sure that your supervisors' supervisors know what you are doing. I had a patient
who does creative design work for a famous industrial laborato-
ry. He does not take the time to write up his own reports for his
company's marketing efforts. He remains anonymous. If you
have a supervisor who gets nervous when he hears that you are
capable and have initiative, size up the situation. If he has a

vested interest in keeping you down or stealing the credit from you, move.

11. *Become involved.* Pick a trade or a position which is something that you can value. If your qualifications are temporarily routine, then go into a company, industry, or institution that is performing work that you can take pride in.

12. *Have a parachute.* There are some people who get very uptight when I advise that the best way to handle a job which makes them unhappy is to quit. They feel that this is the irresponsible counsel of a well-heeled private practitioner. I took the risk of going into private practice because I had saved sufficient money to tide me over in an emergency. People very often have more optional funds than they are aware of. It is vital that you have a number of months' expenses available in cash so that you can meet emergencies, one of which is getting fired or laid off or deciding to quit. If you have a bigger house, an expensive wife, and more children than you can afford, you lack emotional common sense. Have a parachute. Cut down on your expenses. You do not have to remain in an unnecessarily frustrating position which ruins your peace of mind if you have the wherewithal to survive while you look around.

13. *Know your identity.* Is the job a reasonable extension or expression of your personality? Employment stress results when the requirements of the position are unsuitable for a person with your temperament, values, style of approaching problems, and preference for the kinds of social interactions with which you are comfortable. It will be useful for you to reread the section on "Dimensions of Job Suitability" on pages 173–174. Then write down a brief self-description of aspects of your *working personality,* specifically assets and weak spots. After making a list of your "pluses" and "minuses," take the time to write a description of a "suitable" position and an "unsuitable" position. You can use this to compare your present position, and see whether it comes close to a "suitable" or "unsuitable" position. Second, if you are not now employed, or you decide to move on, you can more effectively evaluate and ask questions about any potential jobs.

14. *Diagnose your employment stress.* Review the signs of stress that are common in the working place. Do you have any of them? Do they seem worse while you are working? Have

they developed or become more uncomfortable since you took your present job, or after conditions changed? If so, then you owe it to yourself to either try to create changes in your working conditions or to seek new employment.

15. *Continue to grow.* The fact that you are reading this book indicates that you are the kind of person who wants to improve his/her life. Have you been in the same position for several years? Has the nature of the duties changed? Are you in a situation in which there are some new challenges, new facts developed, new techniques required, and new faces to be met. If not, consider a transfer, a new job, working for a promotion, a vacation. Anything. But change!

19) Creativity and Productivity

"*I am always doing what I can't do yet in order to learn how to do it.*"
(Vincent van Gogh)

"*My interest in natural history has added very little to my sum of achievement . . . [but] it has added immeasurably to my sum of enjoyment in life.*" (Theodore Roosevelt)

"*Creativity has a sense of one's identity imprinted on it.*" (Anonymous workshop participant #1)

"*Get off your ass.*" (Anonymous workshop participant #2)

The twin topics of creativity and productivity can cause as much emotional pain as any other item in this book. On the other hand, their development can create as much pleasure and reassurance as anything else you can do in life. Suffering because of inability to express oneself is avoidable. The lonely, depressed, and unfulfilled person could change his mood through developing his creative potential. Creativity in the service of autonomy is more than the flowering of our potential. Creativity's contribution to autonomy makes us less vulnerable to loneliness, rejection, frustration, and all the other feelings which develop through overreliance on the emotional bounty of others.

Here is how some people react to problems of creativity-productivity:

• "I am a great procrastinator. I do things that can wait."

• "I lack self-discipline. I decide that I'm going to start at a certain time and then I go somewhere."

• "I fear not being considered a success."

• "If no one sees my work, it doesn't exist."

• "I can't express myself properly. Then I cry."

MYTHS

There are a number of common misapprehensions about creativity that prevent people from developing it and then enjoying their own creations.

1. *You must be a genius to be creative.* I used to believe this myself, until I looked up "creativity" in a marvelous invention called the dictionary. Creativity means to bring something into existence. Therefore, the person who bakes a loaf of bread or knits a pair of mittens or makes a table can experience himself/ herself as "creative."

2. *The only fit reward is the Nobel Prize, Oscar, or something comparable.* I know a man who disliked himself because he didn't write. Finally, he began to be productive, and had a quite small piece accepted for publication. When I said to him, "I understand you had a triumph," he replied, "Well, it was only a small triumph." He was happy when I replied, "Not every triumph has to be a major triumph."

3. *If it is not a commercial success, the product is nothing.* This ignores the pleasure of many creative acts. It also ignores the difficulty of selling any creative product. The reasons for rejection may have very little to do with its merit. I think that I have received more pleasure in taking, selecting, and showing my flower photographs to my friends than from five published books. This despite the fact that I think my portfolio has considerable cash value and I have sold very few pictures. The *process* has meant a great deal for my spirits; I am comfortable with the possibility that I may never sell any more photographs.

4. *Suffering makes people creative.* How many people have I known who abused themselves because they did not write or compose or whatever! They tortured themselves for not producing what they believed was in them. The truth of the matter is that most of them were *self-indulgent*. It is foolish to set major goals when you are not ready to follow reasonable steps to get there. Such people often have neurotic problems which keep them from doing what they want to do. Curiously, they consider themselves to be hidden geniuses. My advice to them? "If you are not ready to write (or something else), don't. Enjoy your life, until you are ready."

THE SOURCES OF CREATIVE BLOCKS

My experience suggests that creative blocks can be a symptom of any one of the emotional problems we have already discussed. Therefore, recognizing why your creativity is stifled or reduced can be an important step in emotional development, i.e., in substituting emotional common sense for self-destructiveness.

• *Unclear identity.* If you are unsure of who you are, of your distinctive and deeply experienced qualities, then what you express can be unoriginal, or your ideas will not flow freely.

• *Lack of motivation.* The idea of being famous may be an implant from your family or teachers. Your real potential may be very different. Perhaps, on the other hand, it may be too painful to give up dependency, make sacrifices, and lose other advantages of your present lifestyle.

• *Lack of direction.* You do not have clearly formulated goals, i.e., you do not experience clearly the kind of creative product you want to produce, or you don't know why you should make sacrifices, or what difference success would really make in your life.

• *Lack of preparation.* The first edition of this book took three months, during which time I earned a living and had some fun. But there were years of thinking about these problems, reading, and making notes from groups. This second edition (despite the advantage of some retained text) took twice as long because I felt that some sections needed the benefit of current scientific research.

• *Lack of autonomy.* The need for approval or company can be the death of inspiration or productivity. There is only one eye behind a camera lens or one hand on the paintbrush. If you need encouragement, seek creative acts in groups, like choral singing.

• *Unfinished business.* You can sabotage yourself by trying to fight with, or please, people from your past. Some people with creative blocks are masochistic (see Chapter 1), i.e., they maintain themselves in unproductive condition to demonstrate how their parents mistreated them. Others fear success because they think they will lose support by gaining prestige (see Chapter 17).

• *Belief in your incompetence.* Some people are trained to see themselves as unsuccessful, and therefore they will not attempt anything requiring the approval of others.

• *Vulnerability and high anxiety.* There is an optimal level of arousal (alertness) which permits maximal creativity. Drowsiness is at one extreme, and anxiety at the other; most of us move away from the level of alertness at which we function the best. Creative people often act to change their consciousness in the direction of greater efficiency (Martindale, 1977–78).

IMPROVING CREATIVITY

1. *There is no substitute for hard work.* With hardly any exceptions, the greatest painters, writers, and composers have worked day and night. They buried themselves in their work. Despite Darwin's marvelous scholarship between the ages of twenty-two and twenty-nine which led to the publication of the preliminary report of his findings, *Zoology of the Voyage of the Beagle*, he then delayed publishing *The Origin of the Species* for nineteen years (1859). He referred to only thirteen months and ten days of "hard labor" on the manuscript itself. Arthur Rubinstein says that if he does not practice the piano for one day, he knows it; if he does not practice for two days, his agent knows it; and if he doesn't practice for three days, the public knows it. If you are unable to work hard, then enjoy your life, *forget your impossible dream.*

2. *Know yourself. Believe that creativity is an expression of your identity.* Creativity is also supported or opposed by your individual style, temperament, and attitudes. Taking on a large creative task requires that you estimate your self-discipline, whether you prefer to work alone or with others, how much recognition you require as a reward, and whether you can keep working if the project will be long delayed. Self-awareness can be illustrated in the example of the great conductor Bruno Walter, who was known to be decent in his treatment of his musicians at a time when "dictators of the baton" were generally ruthless and humiliating: ". . . My all too selfless empathy in others critically reduced the assurance and energy of my self-assertion. Eventually, however, it was my very recognition of this moral impediment that showed me the way most accessible

to my nature. I realized that I was certainly not cut out to be a ruler or despot, but rather to be an educator. My task was . . . to uphold my own ideals uncompromisingly without violation of other people's" (Walter, 1957. p. 118)

3. *Get immersed in your project.* When you have experienced and studied many aspects of the area which interests, nay, fascinates you, something new and perhaps great will emerge. Don't worry at first about the "impossible" task of getting a handle on all of it. The very great advantage of looking in many directions, and being open to various aspects of your work, is that new relationships will appear, while trivia will be identified for elimination. A sense of power in controlling your material will develop. Consider the career of Alfred Wegemer, who devised the great concept of continental drift, which now is used to explain the shape of the continental formation of islands, volcanoes, and earthquakes (under the label of "plate tectonics"). He was the Darwin of geology. While he was considered only an amateur geologist by professors of his day, he was an "interdisciplinary investigator" of talent and vision who surely qualifies for a niche in the pantheon of great scientists (Hallem, 1975).

4. *Don't be afraid of inconsistencies.* Your originality and challenge will come from resolving what is apparently irreconcilable. In creativity, oil and water do mix! Another comment by Hallem about Wegemer, who was half a century before his time, is relevant: "He had sufficient breadth of knowledge to seek out and perceptively evaluate supporting evidence from a variety of disciplines . . . [having] discovered weaknesses and inconsistencies [in the accepted model of what the earth was like]." Einstein's work has been described as *integrating opposite concepts simultaneously* (Rothenberg, 1979). Creativity is often a balance between the forces of rational and nonrational thinking in the creator (Douglas, 1977). "Let your mind run free: Trying to make a work fit a preconceived idea often produces what artists call a creative block" (Safan-Gerard, 1978).

Here is how Hans Selye puts it: "There are two ways of detecting something that no one has yet seen; one is to aim at the finest detail by getting as close as possible with the best available analyzing instruments; the other is merely to look at things from a new angle where they show hitherto unexposed facets" (Selye, 1976).

5. *Let your goal be achievement or originality, not fame.* You will create something of value to yourself when your work is related to your real needs, deeply felt values, and the means of satisfying them through achievable goals. Some people are dominated by childhood traumas and set goals which are beyond their capacities or which meet the needs of their parents rather than themselves. (See the chapter on "The Impossible Dream," in Parker, *Effective Decisions and Emotional Fulfillment.*)

The riskiest goal is to be famous or glamorous. This is an insidious form of dependence on the opinions of others. If secretly you wish to be famous, then I suggest that the best path is through meritorious achievement. Even so, you will pay the price of sacrificing family, friends, and fun. Let us listen to Albert Einstein: "The only way to escape the personal corruption of praise is to go on working. One is tempted to stop and listen to it. The only thing is to turn away and go on working. Work. There is nothing else."

6. *Create an overall plan.* The best way to achieve economy of time, effort, and money is to see the picture as a whole before you begin. The initial framework can be modified as your ideas evolve and external circumstances change. With an outline, you can work on one idea when bogged down in another. You can see relationships, repetitions, irrelevant material, and in this way make progress concisely and logically.

How did I write my first book, *Emotional Common Sense?* The original idea came a year before I started to write. Then, a patient was complaining to me about a writing block. When I advised her that a few pages a day would amount to a completed manuscript in a reasonable time, I realized I could take this advice myself. That was Monday. Thursday I wrote my first chapter from 10:00 P.M. to 1:00 A.M. I cleared my desk and started to select chapter headings. I organized notes I had taken at workshops. I looked into my library for relevant material that would add great ideas. As I proceeded, I deleted, added, and changed the order from what was originally intended. Some chapter outlines would be revised four times before I started writing, or even changed in the middle of the writing.

7. *Concentrate your efforts.* There is no substantial, worthwhile project that you can achieve unless you control and limit your investment of extraneous time. Limit the number of pro-

jects that you work on simultaneously. It is inevitable that you sacrifice some pleasures and other goals. Respect your limitations of time and energy. Concentrate your efforts in the main arena. Shostakovich, the premier Soviet composer, had this to say: "I'll admit that writing doesn't always come, but I'm totally against walking around looking at the sky when you're experiencing a block, waiting for inspiration to strike you. Tchaikovsky and Rimski-Korsakov didn't like each other and they agreed on very few things, but they were of one opinion on this: You had to write constantly. If you can't write a major work, write minor trifles. If you can't write at all, orchestrate something. I think Stravinsky felt the same" (Shostakovich, 1979).

8. *Select priorities.* Determine which projects are important and which must be eliminated as inconsequential. Then, if you are to be an achiever and not a frustrated dreamer, you must perform valued activities and eliminate those activities which do not forward your plan. Different people can undertake different numbers of projects simultaneously. Know your own limit! You will accomplish nothing unless you can decide what is important to you and refuse to spend much time on what is time-wasting or distracting. This includes lovers, family, TV, and pleasure-loving friends. If you don't want to make these sacrifices, you have my permission to give up the project and enjoy your life. Don't suffer needlessly.

9. *Develop a balanced attitude toward criticism.* If everybody agrees with something I say, I assume that it is wrong. Life is too complicated to be explained in simple-minded terms. Truth and creativity challenge others in their complacency. The most important difference between people who succeed and those who don't is the self-confidence of the successful ones. The self-confident person strikes out boldly, plans for success, takes risks, and overcomes obstacles. The person with low self-esteem thinks like a failure and does not begin to cope with obstacles. Rather he tries to avoid failure, which is not a recipe for success. I concur with the Russian director and actor Meyerhold (as quoted by Shostakovich, 1979, p. 82): "If the production pleases everyone, then consider it a total failure. If, on the other hand, everyone criticises your work, then perhaps there's something worthwhile in it. Real success comes when people argue about your work, when half the audience is in raptures and the

other half is ready to tear you apart." (Honesty requires that I report that Meyerhold, a man of convictions, disappeared in a Stalinist purge.)

10. *Create the proper atmosphere.* There is a particular ambiance which will enhance your creativity. It takes some time for ideas to incubate and to prepare for worthwhile output (Safan-Gerard, 1978). Therefore, you may need a quiet place, an uninterrupted period of time, and adequate space. My policy: If others interfere with my ability to be creative, I create pain for them or tell them to get lost. If your needs are legitimate and you pursue them without trampling others' rights and productivity, then be forthright in creating that atmosphere in which you can work. It is true, that some "great" people have been brutal in their treatment of others if it was necessary to accomplish their work. I myself seek hours of uninterrupted time, and often work after 11:30 P.M. in order to avoid interruptions. I tolerate my fatigue during the opportunity to be uninterrupted. Anybody who calls after that time does not get a cordial welcome.

11. *Divide the project into parts.* It is very easy to be overwhelmed by the amount of effort required in any worthwhile project. After I completed my Ph.D., I felt that *even I couldn't conceive of the total amount of effort it had taken,* particularly when I took into consideration the cooperation of numerous other people. What if a project seems overwhelming? One man became bogged down in a large doctoral dissertation. What enabled him to make a breakthrough was my suggestion that he decide in advance how much work he could put in on a given day without strain. He said, "One hour." I advised him to work one hour in the morning and one hour in the evening and to enjoy the rest of the day. By working only that amount of time in which you can be productive, you will be able to get going. Gradually you will enjoy yourself and increase your productive hours to a level you would have regarded as impossible. Whether it is a set number of hours, or writing a certain number of pages, or practicing a difficult section of a sonata, know your limits, respect them, and then stop.

12. *Obtain criticism.* Feedback concerning your work can be useful. An open mind has various advantages. At the beginning is the most important time to gain the opinions of others. As you

develop your project, others may be able to point out facets that you did not know about or pitfalls in your intended procedures. Choose individuals who will give you objective comments. Sometimes, useful criticism can even be obtained from those who are basically negative characters or poorly intentioned. I don't like criticism, but I have disciplined myself to listen if I feel that there may be some truth in the message. After you have committed your resources and time, it is less useful to gain basic insights unless you have actually blundered.

13. *Have fun*. The brain turns off at a certain point. Don't push yourself to the point of resenting your sacrifice because you have become totally unproductive owing to boredom, stress, and fatigue. Better yet, don't be a dull dog!

14. *Take a pledge for action*. You want to be creative, be so now. I can suitably conclude this section on creativity with a quotation from Harold Lamb's *Charlemagne*. "Do not wait for an age of perfect minds. It will never come."

20) If All Else Fails: Choosing a Psychotherapist

To conclude a book on emotional development with a chapter on psychotherapy is not a renunciation of what has gone before. Rather, it is a recognition that sometimes external assistance is needed to speed the process. It may be self-destructive to suffer unnecessarily when professional assistance is available. It is also true that participating in some "psychotherapeutic" experiences is by itself self-destructive!

Moreover, many people who seek psychotherapeutic consultation are in my experience very passive. *You can use the ideas of this book to guide your psychotherapist, and also to evaluate whether he or she is having a constructive influence on your life.* I have had many clients who relied on me to determine for them what the content of a session would be. In order not to waste their time, I might suggest a theme, or read them my notes from our last meeting.

Effective use of psychotherapeutic consultation requires that you have some idea as to the causes of emotional pain in your life, and a decision on what areas are of the greatest priority. Then you can honestly say to your psychotherapist, "I am hiring you to help me with a certain job. I know what I want. I also know that I don't want you to be the Great Authority telling me what to do with my own personal life. Let's work together. If we like and respect each other, I will expect progress at a good rate. If I do not have confidence in you, or I do not feel better pretty soon, I will discharge you and seek consultation from somebody else."

You can use this book to learn a great deal about the vocabulary and grammar of your personality. This self-understanding can be worth hundreds and thousands of dollars of saved psychotherapeutic fees.

People enter psychotherapy for one basic reason: *They want to feel better.* To clarify your thinking, this can be broken down:

• *Symptom relief* addresses anxiety, tension, depression, sexual problems, and the like.

• *Situational problems* involve marriage conflicts, entering single life after divorce, employment stress, and so forth.

• *Personal development* encourages the development of one's inner resources, self-reliance, and autonomy.

People frequently enter therapy to obtain situational or symptom relief, and then may leave. Sometimes they see that their life can be more fulfilled, and they continue consultation. Sometimes well-functioning people choose to begin their work on personal development because they realize that they have unused potential or that their life is empty.

Choosing a competent consultant is difficult, because success depends upon many conditions which are hard to measure and predict. In any event, because of the confidential nature of a psychotherapeutic relationship, it is difficult to know what a therapist's track record really is.

Moreover, the definition of psychotherapy, legally and technically, is quite vague, so that it is possible for incompetents, crooks, and charlatans to practice and mistreat or exploit their clients.

What is psychotherapy? It is a means of changing behavior by primarily verbal influence, without the use of medicines or physical agents, so that the individual can enjoy his life more or be free of emotional distress. Psychotherapy is based upon different theories of motivation, emphasizing the effects of early experience and changing our reactions to various situations. The chief agent is a therapist or a therapeutic group.

What is behavior modification? This is an approach to particularly disabling symptoms, e.g., phobias, anxieties, tension. It generally uses techniques which evolved in the psychological study of how learning takes place. There is less emphasis on the significance of the emotional relationship between the client and the therapist. A variety of agents may be used: information about bodily functioning during stress, tension, and anxiety (biofeedback); muscular relaxation; hypnosis; and the use of images to desensitize the patient against fear-provoking ideas and events. A particular symptom may be the chief area of attention, and the consultation terminated when the distress is removed. I have used behavior modification in conjunction with longer-term psychotherapeutic experiences as well as for more sharply focused work. With the proper client, behavior modification can provide effective relief *more rapidly* and *far more cheaply* than psychoanalysis or other forms of verbal, exploratory psychotherapy.

Warning. No system of psychotherapy, and no individual psychotherapist, is equally effective for all individuals or all kinds of problems. When you consult a psychotherapist, be certain you are comfortable with him/her, and that what he is proposing to do is appropriate and is not more expensive than equally good (or better) service you can receive elsewhere. It's your personal head. *Be careful who tampers with it.* (Studies of psychotherapeutic casualties include those of Baekeland and Lundwall, 1975; Chess and Thomas, 1973; Bergin, 1975; Saul, 1972; Strupp, 1976; Parker, 1976; and Tennov, 1975).

Who does psychotherapy? The potential consumer of psychotherapy finds himself in a morass bounded on one end by a wide variety of well-trained professionals and on the other by psychopathic exploiters hiding under the camouflage of cult groups. There are also commercial enterprises like est. The recognized, generally licensed professions are clinical psychology, psychiatry, social work, and psychiatric nursing. There are some other well-trained individuals who for legal reasons are not licensable, and must present themselves as psychotherapists or counselors. Some of this group offer competent service but, generally speaking, are not qualified to receive reimbursement from insurance companies, may not have malpractice insurance, and are not under the control of professional and state ethics and professional conduct committees.

Psychotherapy can be hazardous! Even if you have made a prudent decision to enter psychotherapy, there is no guarantee that you will improve your emotional well-being, or come out unscathed. It could cost you a fortune, cause you to become suicidal, wreck your marriage or employment, or kill your good spirits for years to come. The risks increase when you seek aid from a less well-trained person. However, even the most prestigious licensed practitioner can make mistakes. His very approach to you can be damaging. Psychological researcher Allen E. Bergin queries whether every psychotherapist should have a sign over his door that reads, "Psychotherapy may be harmful to your mental health." He notes in a survey of well-designed studies of psychotherapy that only 5 percent of the untreated individuals got worse, while 10 percent of those in psychotherapy did. My own survey of therapy and encounter groups showed "casualty" rates as high as 19 percent of the participants (Parker, 1976).

AVOIDING HARMFUL PSYCHOTHERAPY

Wrong technique, wrong therapist, wrong patient. Therapeutic success is very complicated. It involves what the therapist expects of the patient, degrees of similarities in background and attitudes, and the patient's degree of independence. This being so, self-destructiveness can be observed in psychotherapy. Prominent psychoanalyst Otto Kernberg (cited by Tennov, 1975, p. 153) refers to the "damaging" therapist (mis-) matched with a patient who has a "deep need" to destroy his/her chances to survive. If you are sufficiently masochistic, you can even find a therapist to grease the skids!

There are a great variety of therapeutic theories, procedures, and therapists' personalities. While there is no research demonstrating that one school of therapy is better than another, experience does teach that if you are fortunate enough to be matched with the correct therapist using well-judged techniques you can improve your well-being. On the other hand, if the therapist rigidly adheres to one theory or procedure, applying the same stale ideas to everyone, you have a good chance of being emotionally damaged, or at the least wasting time, money, spirit, and confidence in gaining future assistance. Some approaches are too *psychologically intense* for people with emotional weaknesses to handle. Perfectly good psychological approaches might be *inappropriate* in special conditions, e.g., psychosomatic complaints.

My candidate for the world's worst treatment. One guess. Psychoanalysis. I have had more patients in my office who wasted large sums of money in psychoanalysis and had failed than in any other form of treatment. This is outrageous, you say. Psychoanalysis, devised by the revered master Sigmund Freud (deceased 1939), has the most prestige and is the most costly, widely practiced form of psychotherapy. I say, What a pity. My observation of psychoanalytic practice is that it hasn't kept up with modern research, that it's full of pitfalls, that an unhealthy proportion of its practitioners are hero worshippers, that it emphasizes what is going on inside your head and in the consultation room to the exclusion of the Real World, and that if the Federal Trade Commission were to investigate its cost-benefit ratio the commissioners would commit suicide because of guilt feelings for having ignored the problem for so long. (If you want some disturbing studies of the problem, read Dorothy Tennov's book and Leon J. Saul, and others in the same volume, Wolman, 1972.)

Because of the rigidity of psychoanalytic technique and theory over the years and the attempt to copy it by individuals who themselves are not properly qualified psychoanalysts, its potential for error has (as has that of every "school" of therapy) overflowed beyond its own banks.

Beware

- Therapist detachment and silence under the guise of objectivity
- Therapist grandiosity in knowing what is best for you under the guise of "intensive training"
- Therapist exploitativeness and creation of dependence under the guise of reliving early conflicts (regression)
- Therapist exaggeration of trivial details of the sessions under the guise of projecting your parental figures
- Enormous fees and excessive sessions under the guise that high payments increase your motivation
- Avoiding real problems under the guise of the importance of the unconscious and the analysis of defenses
- Rejection of your complaints under the guise that the analyst has been analyzed, so by definition you are the nut
- Overinterpretation of your dreams, ideas, and fantasies under the guise that marriage, job, and community problems are not within the scope of psychoanalysis
- Setting goals for you which ignore not only reality but your constitution, temperament, and real-life situation under the guise that "My textbooks and supervisors know far better than you what is good for you"
- Setting standards of improvement which are unrealistic under

the guise that "The therapist is God and therapy can solve everything."

More Therapist Errors, Anyone?

- Demands for deep revelations which could disturb you
- Refusal to make a referral when the treatment goes nowhere
- Greater emotional closeness than the patient can usefully bear
- Emotional blackmail that you will fall apart if you leave the Master
- Not suggesting economical forms of treatment such as group psychotherapy, short-term counseling or crisis intervention, biofeedback, relaxation techniques, which are probably just as effective in many cases.

The Patient Talks Back

- "Week after week the doctor wouldn't say anything. The day I lost my job I saw him. He said, 'I'm surprised you haven't lost it sooner.' I told him, I don't think I will be able to pay you, could you extend credit to me? He said no. I made out a check for that session, threw it at him, and left after eight years."
- "When I was in therapy, I was too dependent. Somehow you have to do it yourself."
- "I believe the therapist who doesn't bind people to him longer than is necessary will never grow as rich as many analysts do, because they can keep you coming for many years and so greatly increase their bankbooks at the same time doing you no good. . . .

"My best advice to fellow seekers of help would be to first of all have some idea of the type of therapy they wish to get. *I would never again* give a therapist carte blanche to do with me what he willed. I'd question him about his methods, fees, background, or anything else that should concern a consumer of his services. Therapists seem to create a certain mysterious aura around exactly what they do and who they are; and it is a patient's right to know certain basic things about a therapist. If a therapist is evasive or can't answer questions, this is something to consider. As to the question of medication, I can only say beware, because the M.D.'s are accustomed to prescribing very readily; and let me tell you that for every medicine a patient pops there are side effects, some very serious and long-ranging, some irremediable."

SELECTING A THERAPIST

The perfect therapist cannot be described. All that you can do is use emotional common sense in selecting among these criteria.

1. *Training.* Look for a recognized degree in one of the mental health professions, i.e., the Ph.D. in psychology; the M.D., including suitable psychiatric training; the M.S.W. in social work, plus special psychotherapeutic training; and the R.N., or clinical specialist, with adequate training to undertake psychotherapy. Your consultant—remember *you* are hiring *him* or *her*, not the other way around—should have training in both the mental and the physiological areas, or some important problems may be mishandled.

2. *Credentials.* Most mental health practitioners are licensed in their own profession, although this may vary from state to state. Where there are no licensing laws, state associations may maintain ethical and professional standards. Additional credentials are board certifications in psychiatry, or in clinical psychology or counseling psychology. Graduation from a training institute is insufficient proof of competence. The warmth, interest, and genuineness of your therapist are most important, particularly his/her ability to understand you and to select an approach suitable to your personal needs. Remember: No one "school" has been so good (including my own) that it can drive out all the others!

3. *Personal psychotherapy.* Absolutely. It is an act of humility to accept that one's weaknesses require a little adjustment. Beware of this: Frequently graduates of psychotherapeutic and psychoanalytic training institutes consider their work to be "didactic analyses," i.e., for training purposes. Therefore, they sometimes have put up a front in order to impress *their* analysts, who are members of the training staff, i.e., have a big say in whether they get their certificates. Conclusion: Personal psychotherapy means nothing unless the therapist relates to you in a pleasant, genuine, helpful, caring way. Research indicates that it is qualities such as these which must be added to proper training in order to produce a good therapist.

4. *Appropriate experience and background:* Training could

have been with the wrong type of patient. The therapist fresh from a job at a mental hospital may be more sympathetic to the needs of the severely disabled than to more functional individuals. Some people prefer therapists of their own sex. Others want somebody with a similar cultural or ethnic background. I do not believe that this is generally necessary, but if you feel that way, try to get a suitable individual if you think it will reduce your resistance to beginning.

5. *Should you go to a clinic?* Maybe, but there are hazards. Your therapist could vary from the most competent to a beginner starting his or her training. Moreover, there may be little economic advantage, since clinic fees may surpass those of some private practitioners who would be glad to consult with you. There is a greater likelihood than in private practice of losing your therapist through his getting fired or going into practice elsewhere.

6. *What about fees?* Fees vary considerably. Sometimes they will be discussed over the telephone, and sometimes you can be invited to come in for a discussion. Some therapists will charge set fees, others will charge according to your ability to pay. You might ask several therapists their fees. You may or may not have to pay for an initial consultation. *Absolutely reject the highest fee.* There is no evidence that competence is correlated with cost. If you are now paying the highest fees of anybody you know, you are reading the right book! (High fees don't equal competence.)

7. *How do I know if I have the right therapist?* I tell my own patients, "If you don't feel better in three months, please leave. I am not the right therapist for you."

CONSUMER'S BILL OF RIGHTS IN PSYCHOTHERAPY AND DYNAMIC GROUPS

You have the right to:

1. Know the practitioner's qualifications. Therefore you may ask him to reveal precisely his training, licensing, experience, personal psychotherapy, and all other information concerning his qualifications to render therapeutic service.

2. Be an active participant in determining the goals for your consultation, whether short-term or extended.

3. Be informed concerning the techniques that will be used, what are their rationales, and what are their hazards.

4. Know whether you will be able to consult with the therapist or the group or encounter leader after hours or after the group experience, should you experience any emotional distress.

5. Know whether the information you reveal will be held in confidence, and what safeguards exist to ensure this. The legal statutes vary from state to state and profession to profession.

6. Be assured that all members of a group will be treated equally, and one person's treatment will not be at the expense of another, or of the entire group.

7. Be informed in advance as to your commitment in money and time before entering a therapeutic relationship or encounter group.

8. Leave an emotionally distressing experience regardless of the commitment in number 7.

9. Know whether physical violence, abuse, sex, or psychedelic drugs are encouraged or condoned during the group or individual session.

SOME SUITABLE PERSONAL QUALITIES OF THE THERAPIST

1. *Broad personal experience.* The therapist ought to be empathetic to your lifestyle and be aware of current events, scientific developments, and social conditions that affect your well-being.

2. *Self-awareness.* Since psychotherapy is often an intense emotional experience for both parties, the therapist should understand how his feelings are affecting you and the therapeutic process.

3. *Accepting attitude.* The therapist ought to be relatively free of prejudices and permissive of others' need to express their doubts and anger to him personally. Punitiveness is not acceptable.

4. *Emotionally expressive.* The therapist ought to be able to feel and express warmth, liking, interest, respect, support, and compassion, as well as anger, fear, and resentment when appropriate.

5. *Personal security.* His self-esteem and ability to function should be independent of excessive needs for approval from his patients.

6. *Intelligence.* Not necessarily a genius, he should be shrewd enough to see through manipulations, able to read between the lines of emotional communications, and alert enough to keep abreast of the professional literature in the area of your problem.

7. *Ethical and dependable.* The patient has a right to expect that his therapist be non-exploitative emotionally and economically, that he be trustworthy in a crisis, consistent, and capable of maintaining confidentiality. Incidentally, most reports of sex between therapist and patient indicate emotional damage to the patient. So beware.

Postscript

It has been a long road down the paths of self-destructiveness and upward toward self-fulfillment. I hope that through recognizing in yourself some of the descriptions, you will use this book as a guide toward fulfillment and emotional common sense and away from self-destructiveness. I have the special pleasure of knowing that through writing I can share the experiences of the many people I have known in my personal life, my professional practice, and in my workshops and lectures with an even larger number. I hope that you will find this material useful for your own personal development.

Bibliography

Abramson, L. Y., and Sackheim, H. A. "A paradox in depression: Uncontrollability and self-blame." *Psychological Bulletin,* 1977, 84(5), 838–851.

Adler, Alfred. *What Life Should Mean to You.* New York: Grosset & Dunlap, 1931.

Akiskal, H. S., and McKinney, W. T. "Depressive disorders: Toward a unified hypothesis." *Science,* October 5, 1973, 182, 21–28.

Andreassi, J. L. *Psychophysiology: Human Behavior and Physiological Responses.* New York: Oxford University Press, 1980.

Arbman, Holger. "Bronze Age Seen in Granite." *Natural History,* 1964, 72, 36–43.

Arieti, Silvano. "Psychotherapy of severe depression." *American Journal of Psychiatry,* 1977, 134(8), 864–868.

Baekeland, F., and Lundwall, L. "Dropping out of treatment: A critical review." *Psychological Bulletin,* 1975(5), 738–783.

Bakal, Donald A. "Headache: A biopsychological perspective." *Psychological Bulletin,* 1975(3), 82, 369–382.

Bakan, P. "Dreaming, REM sleep and the right hemisphere: A theoretical integration." *Journal of Altered States of Consciousness,* 1977–78, vol. 3(4), 285–307.

Beach, Frank A. "Behavioral endocrinology: An emerging discipline." *American Scientist,* 63, March–April, 1975.

Beck, A. T. *The Diagnosis and Management of Depression.* Philadelphia: U. of Pennsylvania Press, 1973.

Beck, A. T. and Young, J. E. "College blues." *Psychology Today,* September 1978, 80–92.

Bergin, Allen E. "When shrinks hurt: Psychotherapy can be dangerous." *Psychology Today,* November 1975, 96–100, 104.

Bernstein, Irwin S., and Gordon, Thomas P. "The function of aggression in primate societies." *American Scientist,* 1974, 63(3), 304–311.

Betz, Barbara J., and Thomas, Caroline B. "Individual temperament as a predictor of health or premature disease." *Johns Hopkins Medical Journal*, 1979, vol. 144, 81–89.

Bowlby, J. "Attachment and Loss." *Attachment*. Vol. I of Attachment and Loss Series, 1969. *Separation and Anger*. Vol. II of Attachment and Loss Series. New York: Basic Books, 1973.

Brady, J. V. "Psychophysiology of Emotional Behavior." In Bachrach, A. J. (ed.) *Experimental Foundations of Clinical Psychology*. New York: Basic Books, 1962.

Brown, Barbara. *Stress and the Art of Biofeedback*. New York: Harper & Row, 1977.

Burns, D. "Cognitive therapy: A different approach to the treatment of depression." *Dawns*, 1977, 1(4), 1–4.

Carr, Edward G. "The motivation of self-injurious behavior." *Psychological Bulletin*, 1977, vol. 87(4), 800–816.

Cavalli-Sforza, L. L. "The genetics of human populations." *Scientific American*, 1974, 231, 80–91.

Chauvin, Remy. *Ethology*. Trans. by Joyce Diamanti. New York: International Universities Press, Inc., 1977.

Chess, Stella, and Thomas, Alexander. "Temperament in the normal infant." In Westman, Jack C. (ed.) *Individual Differences in Children*. New York: Wiley Interscience, 1973.

Chessick, R. D. *Why Psychotherapists Fail*. New York: Science House, 1971.

Crews, David. "The hormonal control of behavior in a lizard. *Scientific American*, August 1979, 180–187.

Darlington, C. D. "The origins of agriculture." *Natural History*. May 1970, 46–50.

De Montigny, C. and Aghajanian, G. K. "Tricyclic anti-depressants: Long-term treatment increases responsivity of rat's forebrain neuronis to Serotonin." *Science*, December 22, 1978, 202–1303–1305.

Dittman, Allen T. "The relationship between body movements and moods in interviews." Undated manuscript. *National Institutes of Health, Education, and Welfare*.

Douglas, J. H. "Discovering creativity." *Science News*, April 23, 1977, 268–270.

Elliott, Frank A. "Neurological factors in violent behavior (The dyscontrol syndrome)." Medical, legal and psychosocial aspects on violence in families. *American Academy of Psychiatry and Law*. Philadelphia Symposium, 1976, vol. 4, no. 4, 297–315.

Emde, Robert N., Gaensbauer, T. J., and Harmon, R. B. "Emotional expression in infancy: A biobehavioral study." *Psychological Issues*, 1975, vol. 10 (1).

Frank, J. D. "Nature and functions of belief systems: Humanism and transcendental religion." *American Psychologist*, July 1977, 555–559.

Freedman, Daniel G. "Ethnic differences in babies." *Human Nature*, January 1979, 36–43.

Freud, A. *The Ego and the Mechanisms of Defense*. New York: International Universities Press, 1953.

Friedman, Meyer. "Type A behavior: A progress report." *The Sciences*, February 1980, 10–11, 28.

Furman, Erna. "Filial Therapy." *Basic Handbook of Child Psychiatry*. New York: Basic Books, 1979, vol. III, 149–159.

Gaither, Neal S., and Stein, Barry E. "Reptiles and mammals use similar sensory organizations in the midbrain." *Science*, August 10, 1979, 205, 595–597.

Gardner, Richard A. "Death of a parent." *Basic Handbook of Child Psychiatry*. New York: Basic Books, 1979, vol. IV, 270–283.

Goldenson, R. M. *The Encyclopedia of Human Behavior*. Garden City, N.Y.: Doubleday, 1970.

Glass, David C, and Singer, Jerome E. "Behavioral aftereffects of unpredictable and uncontrollable aversive events. *American Scientist*, July–August 1972, 60, 457–465.

Greden, J. F., Fontaine, P., Lubetsky, M., and Chamberlin, I. "Anxiety and depression associated with caffeinism among psychiatric inpatients." *American Journal of Psychiatry*, 1978, 135(8), 963–966.

Greenberg, Joel. "Memory research: An era of 'good feeling.' " *Science News*, November 25, 1978, 364–366.

Griest, J. H., et al. Undated manuscript from the Department of Psychiatry, Physical Education and Dance, University of Wisconsin, Madison, Wisconsin.

Gurin, Joel. "Chemical feelings." *Science 80*, November-December 1979, 28–33.

Hall, Elizabeth, ed. "A conversation with Jean Piaget and Barbel Inhelder." *Psychology Today*. May, 1970.

Hall, J. A., Rosenthal, R., Archer, D., DiMatteo, M., and Rogers, P. L. "Decoding Wordless Messages." *Human Nature*, April 1978, 68–71.

Hallem, A. "Alfred Wegemer and the hypothesis of continental drift." *Scientific American*, February 1975, 88–97.

Healy, William. "The Most Complex Material in All Nature." In Beck, S. J., and Molish, H. B. *A Reader in Clinical Psychology*. Glencoe, Ill.: The Free Press, 1959.

Henley, Edith D., Moisset, Beatriz, and Welch, Bruce L. "Catecholamine uptake in cerebral cortex: Adaptive change induced by fighting." *Science*, 1973, 180, 1050–1052.

Hirschfeld, R. M. A., and Klerman, G. L. "Personality attributes and affective disorders." *American Journal of Psychiatry*, 1979, 136:1, 67–70.

Huxley, Julian S. "Cultural process and evolution." In Roe, A., and Simpson, G. G. (eds.) *Behavior and Evolution*. New Haven: Yale University Press, 1958, 437–454.

Isaac, Glynn. "The food-sharing behavior of protohuman hominids." *Scientific American*, April 1978, 90–108.

Jacobson, E. *Depression*. New York: International Universities Press, 1973.

Klein, D. F. "Endogenomorphic depression." *Classification and Prediction of Outcome of Depression*. J. Angst (ed.). New York: F. K. Schattauer Verlag.

Klein, Richard G. "Ice-age Hunters of the Ukraine." *Scientific American*, June 1974, 230, 96–105.

Klerman, G. L. "Pharmacological aspects of depression." In Scott, J. P., and Senay, E. C. (eds.) *Separation and Depression*. Washington: American Association for the Advancement of Science, 1973, 69–90.

Klerman, G. L., Endicott, J., Spitzer, R., and Hirschfeld, R. M. A. "Neurotic depressions: A systematic analysis of multiple criteria and meanings." *American Journal of Psychiatry*, January 1979, 136, 57–61.

Kolata, Gina Bari. "Human evolution: Life-styles and lineages of early hominids." *Science*, 1975, 187, 940–942.

Kovaks, M., and Beck, A. T. "Maladaptive cognitive structures in depression." *The American Journal of Psychiatry*, 1978, 135(5), 525–533.

Laughlin, Henry. *The Neuroses*. Washington: Butterworth, 1967.

Lenney, E. "Women's self-confidence in achievement setting." *Psychological Bulletin*, 1977, 84(1), 1–13.

Lewis, Helen Block. *Guilt and Shame in Neurosis*. New York: International Universities Press, 1971.

Linn, L. *Clinical Manifestations of Psychiatric Disorders. Comprehensive Textbook of Psychiatry*, 2nd ed. Baltimore: Williams & Wilkins, 1975, 783–825.

Leung, D., Glagov, M., and Mathews, M. B. " 'Serotonin Depression'—a biochemical subgroup within the affective disorders?" *Science*, February 6, 1976, 191, 478–480.

Lorenz, Konrad. *On Aggression*. Trans. by Marjorie K. Wilson. New York: Harcourt, Brace & World, 1966.

Maas, J. W. Interviewed in *Roche Report: Frontiers of Psychiatry*, June 1, 1976, 1, 22.

Malmquist, Carl P. "Development from Thirteen to Sixteen Years." *Basic Handbook of Child Psychiatry*. New York: Basic Books, 1979, vol. I, 205–22.

Mark, V. H., and Ervin, F. R. *Violence and the Brain*. New York: Harper & Row, 1970.

Martindale, C. "Creativity, consciousness, and cortical arousal." *Journal of Altered States of Consciousness*, 1977–78, vol. 3(1), 87.

Marty, Martin E. "Science versus religion: An old squabble simmers down. *Saturday Review*, December 10, 1977, 29–35.

Miller, Dorothy A. "Evolution of primate chromosomes." *Science*, December 16, 1977, 1116–1124.

Miller, I. W., III, and Norman, W. H. "Learned helplessness in humans: A review and attribution-theory model." *Psychological Bulletin*, 1979, 86(1), 93–118.

Montagu, Ashley. *The Nature of Human Aggression*. New York: Oxford University Press, 1976.

_____. "Human aggression." *The Sciences*, December 1977, 6–11, 30.

Moore, Andrew M. T. "A pre-neolithic farmers' village on the Euphrates." *Scientific American*, August 1979, 62–70.

Myers, David G. "How groups intensify opinions." *Human Nature*, March 1979, 34–39.

Nemiah, John C. "Anxiety Neurosis." *Comprehensive Textbook of Psychiatry*, 2nd ed. Baltimore: Williams & Wilkins, 1975, 1198–1208.

Novaco, R. W. "The functions and regulation of the arousal of anger." *American Journal of Psychiatry*, October 1976, 1124–1128.

Parker, Rolland S. "The patient who cannot express pain." In R. S. Parker (ed.) *The Emotional Stress of War, Violence, and Peace*. Pittsburgh: Stanwix House, 1972a, 71–85.

_____. "Anger, identification, and irrational target selection." In R. S. Parker (ed.) *The Emotional Stress of War, Violence, and Peace*. Pittsburgh: Stanwix House, 1972b, 12–70.

_____. "Ethical and professional considerations concerning high risk groups." *Journal of Clinical Issues in Psychology*, January 1976, 4–19.

_____. *Effective Decisions and Emotional Fulfillment*. Chicago: Nelson-Hall, 1977. (Barnes & Noble/Harper & Row reprint, 1980.)

_____. *Living Single Successfully*. New York: Franklin Watts, 1978. (Cornerstone/Simon & Schuster reprint, 1980.)

Pert, Candace B., Aposhian, D., and Snyder, Solomon H. "Phylogenetic distribution of opiate receptor binding." *Brain Research*, 1974, 75, 356–361.

Petersen, A. C., and Offer, D. "Adolescent development: Sixteen to nineteen years. *Basic Handbook of Child Psychiatry*. New York: Basic Books, 1979, vol. I, 213–233.

Pilbeam, David. "Rearranging our family tree." *Human Nature*, June 1978, 38–45.

Pinel, J. P., Treit, D., and Rovner, L. I. "Temporal lobe aggression in rats." *Science*, 1977, 197, 1088–1089.

Piotrowski, Zygmunt A. *Perceptanalysis*. New York: Macmillan, 1957.

Plutchik, Robert A. "A language for the emotions." *Psychology Today*, February 1980, 68–78.

Reik, Theodore. "Forgiveness and Vengeance" (1928) in *The Compulsion to Confess*. New York: John Wiley & Sons, 1959.

Restak, R. "The origins of violence." *Saturday Review*, May 12, 1979, 16–19.

Robbins, L. H. "Archeology in the Turkana District, Kenya." *Science*, 1972.

Robinson, D. S., Sourkes, T. L., Nies, A., Harris, L. S., Spector, S., Bartlett,

D. L., and Kaye, I. S. "Monamine metabolism in human brain." *Archives of General Psychiatry*, January 1977, 34, 89–92.

Roche Report: Frontiers of Psychiatry. "Why are some depressed patients difficult to treat." April 1, 1979, 9, 1, 2.

Roosevelt, Theodore. "My life as a naturalist." (May 1918) Reprinted, *Natural History*, April 1980, 84–87.

Rothenberg, A. "Einstein's creative thinking and the general theory of relativity: A documented report." *American Journal of Psychiatry*, January 1979, 38–43.

Routtenberg, Aryeh. "Reward system of the brain." *Scientific American*, November 1978, 154–164.

Rule, Brendan Gail, and Nesdale, Andrew R. "Emotional Arousal and Aggressive Behavior." *Psychological Bulletin*, 1976, vol. 83(5), 851–863.

Safan-Gerard, D. "How to unblock." *Psychology Today*, January 1978, 78–86.

Saul, Leon J. "Some problems in psychoanalytic technique." In Wolman, Benjamin B. (ed.) *Success and Failure in Psychoanalysis and Psychotherapy*. New York: Macmillan, 1972, 107–130.

Scarf, Maggie. *Unfinished Business: Pressure Points in the Lives of Women*. New York: Doubleday & Co., 1980.

Scharrer, Berta. "An evolutionary interpretation of the phenomenon of neurosecretion. 47th James Arthur lecture on the evolution of the human brain. *The American Museum of Natural History*, 1977, p. 15.

Schmale, A. H. "Adaptive role of depression in health and disease." In Scott, J. P., and Senay, E. C. (eds.) *Separation and Depression*. Washington: American Association for the Advancement of Science, 1973, 187–214.

Schwartz, G. E. "Undelivered warnings." *Psychology Today*, March 1980, p. 116.

Selye, Hans. *The Stress of Life* (Revised Edition). New York: McGraw-Hill, 1976.

Shabecoff, Philip. "Psychosomatic medicine finds why work can be sickening." *New York Times*, February 3, 1980, 22E.

Shostakovich, Dmitri. *Testimony: Memoirs*, related to and edited by Solomon Volkov. New York: Harper & Row, 1979.

Silverman, P. L. "Some personality correlates of attributive projection." *Perceptual and Motor Skills*, 1963, 17, 947–953.

Solecki, Ralph S. "Shanidar IV, a Neanderthal flower burial in Northern Iraq." *Science*, November 28, 1975, 190, 880–881.

Stekel, Wilhelm. *Sadism and Masochism* (1929). New York: Liveright, 1953, 2 vols.

Strupp, H. L., Hadley, S. W., Gomes, B., and Armstrong, S. H. "Negative effects in psychotherapy." Unpublished manuscript, Vanderbilt University, 1976.

Tallman, J. F., Paul, S. M., Skolnick, P., and Gallager, Dorothy W. "Receptors for the age of anxiety: Pharmacology of the benzodiazepines." *Science*, January 18, 1980, vol. 207, 274–78.

Tanner, Nancy, and Zihlman, Adrienne. "Women in evolution. Part I: Innovation and selection in human origins." *Signs: Journal of Women in Culture and Society*, Spring 1976, vol. 1. (no. 3, part 1), 585–608.

Tec, L. *The Fear of Success*. New York: Signet, 1976.

Tennov, Dorothy. *Psychotherapy: The Hazardous Cure*. New York: Abelard-Schuman, 1975.

Thomas, Alexander, and Chess, Stella. *Temperament and Development*. New York: Brunner/Mazel, 1977.

Thomas, Alexander, Chess, Stella, and Birch, Herbert G. *Temperament and Behavior Disorders in Children*. New York: New York University Press, 1969.

Thorpe, W. H. *Animal Nature and Human Nature*. Garden City, N.Y.: Anchor Press/Doubleday, 1974.

Tiger, L. "Optimism: The biological roots of hope." *Psychology Today*, January 1979, 18–30.

Toffler, Alvin. *Future Shock*. New York: Bantam, 1970.

Tolman, E. "Cognitive maps in rats and man." *Psychological Review*, 1948, 55, 189–208.

Torrance, E. P., and Mourad, S. "Role of hemisphericity in performance on selected measures of creativity. *The Gifted Child Quarterly*, Spring 1979, 44–55.

Van Gogh, Vincent. *Complete Letters*, cited *New York Times*, February 10, 1979, p. 17.

Walter, Bruno. *Of Music and Music-Making*. New York: Norton, 1957.

Wareham, John. *Making the Most Out of Lunch: Techniques for Chairmen When Assessing Job Candidates*. *New York Times*, Sec. 2, January 7, 1979.

Washburn, S. L. "What we can't learn about people from apes." *Human Nature*, November 1978, 70–75.

Washburn, S. L., and Harding, R. S. "Evolution and human nature. In S. Arieti, et al (eds.) *American Handbook of Psychiatry*, 2nd ed., vol. 6. New York: Basic Books, 1975, pp. 1–13.

Westermeyer, Joseph, Bush, Janet, and Wintrob, Ronald. "A review of the relationship between dysphoria, pleasure and human bonding." *Journal of Clinical Psychiatry*, 1978, 39(5), 415–424.

Wilson, Edmund O. *Sociobiology*. Cambridge, Mass.: Belknap/Harvard, 1975.

———. *On Human Nature*. Cambridge, Mass.: Harvard University Press, 1978.

Yankelovich, Daniel, and Barrett, W. *Ego and Instinct: The Psychoanalytic View of Human Nature—Revised*. New York: Random House, 1970.

Young, J. Z. *Programs of the Brain*. New York: Oxford University Press, 1978.

———. "Women and evolution, II: Subsistence and social organization among early hominids." *Signs: Journal of Women in Culture and Society*. Autumn 1978a, vol. 4(1), 4–20.

Zihlman, Adrienne L. "Motherhood in transition: From ape to human." In Miller, W. B., and Newman, Lucille F. (eds.) *The First Child and Family Formation*. Carolina Population Center: The U. of North Carolina, 1978b, 35–50.

Zihlman, Adrienne, and Tanner, Nancy. "Gathering and the hominid adaptation." In Tiger, L., and Fowler, H. (eds.) *Female Hierarchies*. Chicago: Beresford Book Service, 1978, 163–194.

Index